Nation
of
Bastards

NATION
of
BASTARDS

Essays on the end of marriage

DOUGLAS FARROW

FOREWORD BY WILLIAM D. GAIRDNER

BPS Books

Published by BPS Books
Toronto, Canada
www.bpsbooks.net
A division of Bastian Publishing Services Ltd.

ISBN 978-0-9784402-4-4

Cataloguing in Publication Data
available from Library and Archives Canada.

Cover design: Michaela Miron, Kinetics Design
Text design and typesetting: Daniel Crack, Kinetics Design
www.kdbooks.ca

Cover illustration: The Holy Family, Michelangelo,
Michelangelo Buonarroti. Holy Family. (Doni tondo).
Uffizi, Florence, Italy
Photo credit: Scala/Art Resource, NY; used by permission.

To the children

of Rousseau

Contents

Foreword *ix*

Introduction *1*

Death of a Dictum and other misfortunes *7*

On the Half-life of Half-witted Legislation *41*

Nation of Bastards *49*
Musings on Marriage and Freedom

Which Secularism? *85*
Rethinking the Role of Religion in Public Life

Epilogue *111*

Foreword

PROFESSOR FARROW has rendered us all – Christians, non-Christians, agnostics, and yes, even atheists – a public service in publishing this little book. It is a call to action from a deeply aggrieved soul who loves his country even as he mourns it; for, as argued here, our once peaceable kingdom has become a nation of increasingly autonomous individuals severed from the oldest and most important forms of human legitimacy – political, legal, biological, and moral.

Such a heartfelt cry in the Canadian conceptual wilderness reminds me of nothing so much as the many booklets, pamphlets, and tracts published by private Canadian and American citizens during recent centuries, prior to the rise of the homogenized public orthodoxies now suffered on mass publics by mass media. There was a time when concerned citizens took up such writing as a moral and political duty (often at their own expense) in order to ring the change of their most passionate ideas on the public forge. It is a rousing thing to see it here.

In the variety of essays presented, readers will sense the main themes soon enough. Of greatest import, perhaps, is that of the gradual insinuation of state control into the heart of family life, marriage, and the traditional parent–child relationship, all achieved by a species of legal legerdemain that Farrow reveals in intricate detail. What is clear by the end is that none of this would have been possible but for the fact that modern democratic states, so eager to de-legitimize their own religious and moral traditions in the name of equality, have settled on what they believe to be a neutral and tolerant secular ground that in fact operates as a new, this-worldly religion. It is a false political religion that can only sustain itself by demanding the substitution of merely legal relationships for the important biological ties that bind. The recent substitution of the phrase "two persons" for "a man and a woman" in the ancient definition of marriage is the most shocking example. With one stroke this revision has successfully removed procreative biology as a condition for marriage, in order to accommodate and equalize the "marriages" of homosexuals. It is a delight to see how Farrow delicately eviscerates the law and the language surrounding this fateful metamorphosis, showing it to be far from neutral.

Never far from view, either, is the author's justly damning critique of the *Canadian Charter of Rights and Freedoms* (1982), especially with respect to section 15, on so-called equality rights, which are now used far too often as a battering ram to bring down social and economic policies that for good reason were created to protect and privilege human relationships once considered essential to the very survival of society. After pondering Farrow's essays, readers will be pardoned for thinking that there has likely never been as vicious and thoroughgoing an attack on marriage and the family in the name of equality since the days of the French Revolution.

Certainly the most poignant and important concern of this

little book – it ought to concern every caring citizen – is the manner in which the interests of children have been shoved aside to accommodate our new state religion and the demolition of marriage it has required. I don't like the term "rights" at all, for it too is all too often found severed completely from its essential link to obligation. But if there was ever a natural right to be found, it must surely be the right of all children, wherever possible, to know and be raised by their own parents. This book reminds us how, as a nation, we have cavalierly eliminated this universal right of children, merely to satisfy the desires of a small minority of adults who repudiate mutual procreation altogether.

Nation of Bastards explains how the state has commandeered the institution of marriage, how against all truth and logic our courts have declared public morality to be a private matter, and therefore how even human dignity – a concept deeply rooted in our demanding religious and moral tradition – has been thrown overboard in favour of the embarrassingly simplistic and unsatisfying idea of personal autonomy.

I close by saying that I hope the publication of this book will encourage more of the same, because we are presently living in a period of national _Denkverboten,_ as the Germans have called it – the official forbidding of thought. All Canadians feel this worm at work in their hearts whenever they have the urge to speak the truth but keep quiet out of fear. Professor Farrow is not afraid to speak out boldly, and for this we owe him and his book a debt of gratitude.

WILLIAM D. GAIRDNER

William D. Gairdner is the author of eight volumes on social, political, and literary issues, including The Trouble with Canada _and_ The War Against the Family. _He was the founding president of Civitas, and a co-editor of the book_ Canada's Founding Debates.

Introduction

I hope I don't disappoint, but I am not Carolyn Parrish – she of "Damn Americans! I hate those bastards" fame – and these essays are not about America. They are about Canada. What is more, most of them are about an issue that our leading opinion-makers have declared closed, namely, marriage. Closure is wishful thinking, however, as I hope to make clear. My own view is that Canada's divorce from traditional marriage (see Cere and Farrow, eds., *Divorcing Marriage*, McGill-Queen's University Press, 2004) has had just the consequence we should have expected. It has landed us in a nasty custody battle between the state and the natural family unit for the country's children. Americans, of course, can look forward to the same thing if they follow us down the same path.

This custody battle is not only a battle for the hearts and minds of young people, as some may imagine. It is a legal and political battle with implications for every citizen. For marriage is not merely an institution of restraint, essential to the moral fibre and discipline of society. It is also an institution in which society invests some of its most important ideals of freedom. Freedom itself is at stake in the anti-marriage revolution, from which the state will emerge either appropriately humbled before its citizens or dangerously exalted.

Given the urgency of the situation, and the speed with which it is developing, I have decided to publish these essays in a form accessible both to colleagues and to the general public. I am only too conscious of the fact that by themselves they form a meagre contribution, but in such times even a meagre contribution is better than none. At all events, we cannot wait on the large-scale scientific studies that are being designed to examine the long-range effects of our current social experiments, since their results will be available to us only after the most serious damage has been done. It is necessary now to think ahead, to strain to see as far as we can, and to unite across the boundaries of our usual solitudes in order to resist the rapid erosion of our freedom.

A brief comment on the origin of these essays: The first was occasioned by a request from the Robarts Centre for Canadian Studies to write something for a special Trudeau-related issue of *Canada Watch*. The issue never appeared, but the article took on a life of its own, and evolved into its present trilogistic form, as I engaged in public lectures and debates about same-sex marriage. It forms, I think, a suitable companion piece to the title essay, which was presented in 2006 at the National Press Club in Ottawa but began life as a contribution to the 2005 Illuminating Marriage colloquium in Kananaskis, organized by the Institute for the Study of Marriage, Law and Culture. (Watch for a new book from the Institute, *The Conjugal Bond*, comprising much of the work done or begun at Kananaskis.)

Between these two essays I have inserted a journalistic piece that appeared recently in the *Western Standard*, dealing with the three-parents case in Ontario. That case illustrates just how fast things are moving in Canada, and how the *parens patriae* power of the state is being exercised with ever greater abandon. Taken in its larger context, it also suggests that traditional wisdom and traditional liberties – the two go together – are being caught in a kind of pincer movement. While Canada has been busy redefining marriage, parenthood, and the family to fit the demands of people in same-sex relationships, parts of Europe have already moved to exclude people with principled objections to such demands from participation in public life. Witness, for example, the disenfranchising of Roman Catholic adoption agencies in Britain under the Sexual Orientation Regulations (SOR). Similar things are beginning to happen here, north and south of the border.

It is a telling feature of the struggle in which we are now engaged that even the fundamental freedoms of religion and of conscience are being overridden by so-called equality rights, and that policies in support of a fiction called "social diversity" are being used to trample on the actual diversity that is a function of a free society. Prominent figures on both sides of the Atlantic have begun to question the right of parents to educate their children according to their own religious beliefs, lest they render the virgin earth inhospitable to the planting of the homogenizing values of the state. (This is done under the rubric of children's rights, though the same people can often be found promoting the use of eugenic science to interfere even with the building blocks of a child's biology.) Others have begun to question the right of religious organizations to operate freely on a charitable basis, if their teachings and practices do not conform to the current ideology of the state. That the beliefs and practices of these same religions may belong to the founding and progress of the states in question, and lie at the roots of their historic social order, seems hardly to matter. Both society and the state are to be reinvented in the image of the new ideologues and the main sources of resistance must be eradicated. The lordship of the lordless powers (to borrow a phrase from Karl Barth) knows no bounds.

Being a theologian, I have not shied from bringing theological insights to bear on my analysis of the marriage issue and of its political context. Readers who think that odd, or at least antiquated, may consult *Recognizing Religion in a Secular Society* (Farrow, ed., McGill-Queen's, 2004), but I think they will discover even here, if they are thoughtful, that culture, law, and politics are never really a-theological. I have included in the present book a modified version of my essay, "Which Secularism?", previously available only in French (see *La religion dans la sphère publique*, ed. Solange Lefebvre, Université de Montréal, 2005), to reinforce that point, though it touches on marriage only in passing. When the chief justice remarked that Canada is founded on secular principles, she presumably referred not to the founders' principled rejection of theological considerations – that would obviously be counterfactual – but to certain established notions, themselves theological in origin, of a division of duties and powers between church and state. It is not the church or the other religious communities that threaten respect for that division today. It is our courts and parliaments and instruments of public policy that threaten it. This needs to be pointed out in terms at once secular and theological, particularly where marriage is concerned. For marriage is an institution that, properly understood, bridges not only the sexes but also the civil and the religious.

Being a person with little inclination toward the politically correct, and with no respect whatsoever for the cowardice and apathy that today masquerade as the virtue of tolerance, I have also not shied from using a provocative title. But the title is not meant to be pejorative, like Parrish's notorious remark. It is meant to be prophetic: a warning of disenfranchisement, of loss of birthright. If the warning is heeded, the prophecy will fail, as I very much hope it will.

There is, inevitably, some repetition between these pieces, which I trust the reader will forgive. It remains only to say that I am indebted to Bill Gairdner for his generosity in writing the foreword, and to a good many friends in academia and in the law, for whose instruction and support I am very thankful, but who may perhaps be grateful for remaining anonymous here. I am also indebted to the publisher for publishing; that is, for not being anonymous. If "Damn Americans!" is not an appropriate subtitle to this little book, "Damn the torpedoes!" might be. Needless to say, responsibility for the views expressed, and for any errors or infelicities, remains my own.

DOUGLAS FARROW
McGILL UNIVERSITY

Death of a Dictum
and other misfortunes

The idea, then, that the

civil government should,

at its own discretion, penetrate and

pervade the family and the household,

is a great and pernicious mistake.

LEO XIII, *Rerum Novarum* §14

I

Death of a Dictum

IN 1969 Pierre Trudeau's Omnibus Bill C-150 decriminalized sodomy and other forms of private consensual sex. In 2005 Canada legislated same-sex marriage with Bill C-38. There is no straight line, either logically or historically, from the one event to the other. Indeed, viewed from the vantage point of Trudeau's famous dictum that there is no place for the state in the bedrooms of the nation (borrowed from the *Globe and Mail*, but adapted from Pope Leo), these developments appear to be contradictory. For same-sex marriage, as we shall see, requires us to bury that dictum along with the traditional institution. Some critical reflection on our recent history is therefore in order.

In defence of decriminalization Trudeau and his justice minister John Turner, following Britain's 1957 Wolfenden report, appealed to the basic Western distinctions between sin and crime, and between church and state, that had been compromised by the 1533 *Buggery Act*.[1] Sodomy, like other forms of fornication, may be a sin, but sin is a matter of conscience, requiring as a remedy priestcraft not statecraft. The state may have an interest in encouraging stable family life, in protecting the vulnerable, and in suppressing public indecency, but consensual sex privately conducted is not a public matter and it is not the crown's business to concern itself with individual sexual choices.

So the argument went. In making it, the government of Canada, like the British government, adopted a stance more traditional than is sometimes imagined. As Senator Cools noted in the debate on Bill S-10,[2] the Wolfenden report read as follows:

> Unless a deliberate attempt is to be made by society, acting through the agency of the law, to equate the sphere of crime with that of sin, there must remain a realm of private morality and immorality which is, in brief and crude terms, not the law's business. To say this is not to condone or encourage private immorality. On the contrary, to emphasise the personal and private nature of moral or immoral conduct is to emphasise the personal and private responsibility of the individual for his own actions, and that is a responsibility which a mature agent can properly be expected to carry for himself without the threat of punishment from the law.

Obviously it is a long way from the decriminalization of sodomy, justified in these terms, to same-sex marriage. So how did we get to where we are today? Several circumstantial factors must be taken into account, together with the creation of the *Canadian Charter of Rights and Freedoms*, without which the redefinition of marriage could not have taken place.

First, the circumstantial factors. C-150 may have been defended in classical religious terms, but it also reflected the changing scene of the sixties, punctuated later in that year of 1969 by the Stonewall riots. This scene (scripted mainly in the United States) included the sexual revolution, the beginnings of what John Paul II would call the contraceptive mentality,[3] and a drive for deregulation of marriage and of sexual relations generally. Of the middle item we may be content to say the obvious: it was the *sine qua non* for the other two. In his controversial 1968 encyclical *Humanae Vitae*, Paul VI pointed to the link between the contraceptive pill, introduced in 1958, and the increase of what we now call casual sex; that is, in fornication and adultery. He also pointed prophetically to an increase in alienation between the sexes and to the prospect of unheard-of government interventions in human reproduction (of which China now provides one of the most notorious examples).[4] But the accurate predictions of the pope were made the object of ridicule by journalists and commentators.

The fraudulent claims of Alfred Kinsey, on the other hand, were welcomed as a new and liberating gospel. The Kinsey reports (1948 and 1953), which were based on skewed samples and unscientific as well as unethical procedures, told society that its sexual mores and even its laws were out of step with reality. They brought forward the future by claiming that it was already the present. This helped to produce a climate in which the decriminalization of deviant acts was unlikely to cause too great a stir, for it encouraged people to question whether there was much in the way of sexual behaviour between consenting adults that could be called deviant.[5] Not coincidentally, this was also the period of growing demand, fed in Canada by the fires kindled in the Quiet Revolution, for a rigid separation of church and state.

These developments undermined traditional morality and

changed, at first gradually and then more rapidly, both public and private conduct. They also called into question the common understanding of the role of government in keeping public moral order. As I said, Trudeau's dictum did not mean that the state had no business making or endorsing moral judgments, only that it was not its task to enforce those judgments in the realm of private behaviour. "What's done in private between adults doesn't concern the criminal code," he argued; "when it becomes public this is a different matter."[6] But as moral consensus disappeared, Trudeau's dictum began to be interpreted as if morality were itself a matter of private judgment, and as if public order were dependent chiefly on recognition of that.

The enormity of this reversal of historic wisdom, as well as the full extent of its consequences, has yet to be reckoned with. One ironic and unlooked-for (though not unpredicted) consequence has been the advance, rather than the retreat, of the interfering state. But before saying more about that we must take stock of another development of the Trudeau era. I speak of the *Charter*, of course, or more precisely the interpretation of the *Charter* in recent years as the country's main instrument of justice, and of equality rights as the very heart of justice.

Every system of law requires recognition of a moral order – witness the *Charter*'s preamble – and is governed by some conception of justice. Under the conditions of a milieu in which morality is coming to be regarded as a matter of private judgment, as a function of the self-expression of the person rather than as an established parameter of healthy personhood, it cannot surprise us that equality rights should emerge as the only remaining public moral structure and the highest embodiment of justice. And that is what has happened. Section 15 of the *Charter*, on equality rights, has become Canada's governing principle, and the courts rather than the legislatures have become (as on this conception they must) Canada's true seat of government. The *Charter* itself has become the instrument of a subjectivist anthropology in which human dignity is reduced to personal autonomy, such that all things are measured by the *summum bonum* of "free choice"; to which, rather than to the common good, equality rights are now pegged. Were the case otherwise, same-sex marriage would almost certainly not have been imposed on the nation by its courts. Not only because it would be recognized, as by Wolfenden and Trudeau, that the proper business of the law is with persons qua citizens, not with persons qua autonomous choosers,[7] but also because the cost to society of same-sex marriage is simply too high.

To specify but one cost, the recasting of marriage in non-procreative terms – for that is the essential achievement of the new gender-free definition – eliminates the only institution society has that upholds a child's right to the care of his or her own parents. Indeed, it opens to question the legal foundation of the child–parent bond, and of the parental claim to the child over against that of some other party, such as the state. This too, in our haste, we have not even begun to reckon with. C-150's loosening of divorce and abortion laws had many deleterious effects – denied in prospect but demonstrable in retrospect – yet C-150 did not tamper directly with the fundamentals of the human social structure, as current legislation has done. It is not by accident that Bill C-38, in its consequential amendments, dismantles the language of "natural parent," "blood relation-ship," and the like – language that acknowledges implicitly the priority of the family to the state – in favour of terms such as "legal parent" and "legal parent–child relationship." These alterations represent a larger restructuring of Canadian law in such a way as to reduce, not only marriage, but the whole nexus of family relations to the status of a legal construct, thus bringing them under the control of the state and making them subject to whatever definitions the state wishes to impose upon them.

With this tampering, we have witnessed the demise of Trudeau's dictum under the auspices of his *Charter*. The autonomy principle has seized on the *Charter* and deployed it to create (beware divine justice!) a meddlesome state that imagines that it *does* have a place in the bedrooms of the nation. For when we have done with all the purring about human dignity, and all the legal twisting and turning, that is the logic of genderless, procreationless "marriage." The state will be a party, in principle if not in practice, to our sexual partnerships as such. Indeed, the time for the Law Commission's proposal in *Beyond Conjugality* is now rapidly approaching: state registration and regulation of all manner of domestic relations.

II

Theft of a Sacrament

Marriage has been treated, in our society, as a sacrament, whereby two people consecrate their lives not just to each other but to the family that will spring from them. In no sense is marriage, so conceived, merely the rubber-stamping of a sexual contract. It marks an existential transition, a move away from the concerns of one generation towards a concern for the next. It is not an act of gratification but an act of renunciation, the beneficiaries of which are not the spouses themselves, but their future children. Without marriage, as we are beginning to see, societies do not reproduce themselves. Hence to treat marriage as a human toy, that can be redesigned at will and for the pleasure of the merely living, is to jeopardize the rightful hopes of those unborn. Even if gay marriage does not involve perversion, therefore, to defend it is surely perverse.

ROGER SCRUTON[8]

Our old common-law definition of marriage, articulated in *Hyde* v. *Hyde and Woodmansee* (1866) as "the voluntary union for life of one man and one woman to the exclusion of all others," follows that of Roman jurisprudence as formulated by Modestinus in the third century: "Marriage is the union of a man and a woman, a consortium for the whole of life involving the communication of divine and human rights."[9] This understanding of marriage is deeply rooted in Western law and culture and is not merely the product, as some seem to think, of a passing phase of late Christendom.[10] Christianity has reinforced monogamy and offered a systematic interpretation of marriage in terms of the intrinsic goods delineated by

Augustine: *proles, fides, et sacramentum* – that is, procreation or fruitfulness, chastity or faithfulness, and bonding or fellowship. It has also resituated marriage eschatologically, adding a new and deeper sacramental dimension. But the basic conception of marriage is a common and ancient one, belonging to natural law: Marriage is a sexually differentiated union that binds the partners not only to each other but to their offspring. As such, it involves both a renunciation of certain liberties and the assumption of certain rights, rights that marriage itself confers, or that God confers through marriage.

Because the renunciation and the rights are connected to the procreation and protection of children, they are said to be divine as well as human. And, being divine, they cannot be gainsaid by outside parties, not even by the state. For the family unit based on marriage (which, on the Christian view, may even become the domestic church) is by no means a creation of the state. Theologically speaking, it precedes and exceeds the state, though it cannot avoid a kind of mutual responsibility with and to the state. The preamble to the 1960 *Canadian Bill of Rights* recognizes this. It affirms that "the Canadian Nation is founded upon principles that acknowledge the supremacy of God, the dignity and worth of the human person and the protection of the family in a society of free men and free institutions." Note the order: the supremacy of God and the dignity of the person made in God's image hold the first place, the family follows, then civil society and its secondary institutions. This implies that the right "to marry and to found a family," as the *Universal Declaration of Human Rights* has it, is not a right granted by the state but by God. It is a natural right with an *a priori* claim on the state's respect, the state having a responsibility to act in a manner consistent with divine law, human dignity, and the freedom of the family. As Paul Martin Sr said when drafting the *Bill of Rights'* preamble, he hoped for a Canada dedicated to the principles of the *Universal Declaration* "in their human, social, political, economic and legal terms, particularly those concerning the sanctity and inviolability of the family as the fundamental unit of society."[11]

If we are thinking in these terms, we will recognize how dramatically things have changed in Canada. Not only do we have an entirely novel definition of marriage that excludes procreation from its purview. That would be dramatic enough, since, as Professor Scruton says, it shifts the focus of our most basic social institution from inter-generational concerns to those of present personal gratification, and in doing so eliminates many of the responsibilities that belong to marriage. But, together with the novel definition itself, we also have the novel idea that the state has the power to re-invent marriage by adopting and enforcing this definition. By claiming such a power the Canadian state has drawn marriage and the family into a captive orbit. It has reversed the gravitational field between the family and the state, putting itself at odds with the founding principles of Canada and with the notion of free men and free institutions. It has effectively made every man, woman, and child a chattel of the state, by turning their most fundamental human connections into mere legal constructs at the state's disposal. It has transformed those connections from divine gifts into gifts of the state.[12]

I am not sure whether to call this the de-sacralization of marriage or the re-sacralization of the state. Perhaps it is both, for the people's loss is the state's illicit gain. The state rightly takes a regulatory interest in marriage on account of the social goods that attach to it – especially the stability of community and property, of human reproduction and the care of children, and of bonding between the sexes and the generations. It rightly exercises both positive and negative discrimination in favour of marriage (tax breaks being an example of the former, consanguinity laws an example of the latter). But it does not rightly assume the power to redefine marriage, because it is not the author or the mediator of marriage. The state that imagines itself the author of marriage, or thinks that its *Charter* justifies it in assuming control over the very substance of marriage, is a dangerous state with highly inflated religious pretensions.[13]

No doubt this charge will baffle those who suppose that Canada has done what it has done just because it has turned from religious to "secular" values, which is the line taken by the Supreme Court. A good deal of their confusion would be cleared up by reading Professor DeCoste's commentary on the *Reference re Same-sex Marriage*, aptly entitled "Courting Leviathan."[14] DeCoste has exposed the false dichotomy between religious and civil marriage deployed by the court as a device for handing over to the state what does not belong to it. To be sure, it is only marriage "for civil purposes" that has been declared by the court a creature of the state. But what other kind of marriage is there? Marriage may take place in a religious context or a non-religious context. It may be witnessed by the minister of a religious community or by a justice of the peace. But it is the partners who marry each other, not the church or the state who marries them; and wherever they marry, if they marry lawfully, their marriage is marriage for civil purposes. The court's sophistry notwithstanding, it has laid hands on marriage qua marriage and allowed it to mean and to confer nothing but what the state says it is to mean and to confer. Only a state that does not recognize its own limits – the limits imposed on it because it is not the author or arbiter of either family life or religious life – would do such a thing. Only a citizenry that is thoroughly befuddled would allow the state to do it.

If this sounds a bit hard on the court – or on the people's parliamentary representatives, who have done their best to turn stolen property into a gift – consider another fact. On the one hand, the court has falsely divided civil from religious marriage. On the other hand, it has perversely conflated the two opposing views of marriage with which Canada is now confronted. Taking Canadians for fools, it has pretended that these are but variants of one and the same view, and that the new definition represents only a minor modification of the old. To expose this further sophistry it is necessary only to notice that the new court-approved definition jeopardizes all three of the traditional goods of marriage.[15]

We have already observed that marriage as "the lawful union of two persons to the exclusion of all others" is marriage that wants to do without procreation, the first of the intrinsic goods; only thus can it become inclusive of same-sex couples.[16] The absence of "for life" suggests ambivalence about the third good also, especially about the commitment to permanency that is intended to create a climate of trust for the children and for all concerned. Where procreation is no longer a definitive element, and children and grandchildren no longer a primary consideration – where marriage no longer marks a turning from one generation to the next – why should the bonding be permanent? There is no compelling reason to aim at permanency. So, on the new definition, two strands of the threefold marital cord are effectively cut. The other good, *fides*, or faithfulness, is ostensibly retained with the phrase, "two ... to the exclusion of all others," but examination of the theory behind the new definition turns up serious knife marks on this remaining strand as well. Indeed, the theory in question actively subverts the idea that the marital union is an exclusive one.

This is worth reflecting on for a moment. The key to conceiving the institution of marriage sans procreation is an approach called "close-relationship theory." My colleague Daniel Cere has remarked on the dubious origins of this theory, which can be traced back behind the likes of Alfred Kinsey or Margaret Mead to Friedrich Engels, via the failed Soviet experiments pioneered by Aleksandra Kollantai.[17] Its contemporary advocates work, just as they did, with a concept of union that is highly malleable, to say the least. What they seek by way of this theory is "recognition and respect for our chosen relationships in their many forms," a means of accommodating "a wide range of relationships, households, and families."[18] Close-relationship theory does the necessary work. It emphasizes emotional attachment more than the permanent bonding of lives, a feeling of intimacy above chastity or faithfulness, and sexual pleasure over procreation. It interests itself in gratification not renunciation. In short, it offers a radically different account of the nature and function of marriage, and so also of the politics of marriage.

The Supreme Court's denial of this fact is certainly peculiar, if not perverse, as is the reasoning on which it leans. Take for example its response to the argument from traditionalists about the natural limits of marriage as an intrinsically heterosexual institution. Stating the obvious, the court observes that this argument, the point of which is to deny that gay marriage really is marriage, "can succeed only if its proponents can identify an objective core of meaning which defines what is 'natural' in relation to marriage. Absent this, the argument is merely tautological." Fair enough. But then the court goes on to say: "The only objective core which the interveners before us agree is 'natural' to marriage is that it is the voluntary union of two people to the exclusion of all others. Beyond this, views diverge. We are faced with competing opinions on what the natural limits of marriage may be."[19] In other words, we do not have two fundamentally different views of marriage after all. We agree (so we are informed) on the basic fact that marriage is essentially the union of two persons. The problem of natural limits arises only afterwards and quite independently. One variant of our common view of marriage adds no gender stipulation and thus offers a broader, more inclusive perspective, well suited to an open and tolerant society. The other variant does add a gender stipulation and is therefore narrower, and presumably less well suited. The court says that it is not its task "to determine, in the abstract, what the natural limits of marriage must be,"[20] but only to say whether the broader definition is constitutional. It finds that it is.

Now the claim that proponents of traditional marriage and proponents of gay marriage are equally committed to the binary and exclusive nature of marriage already stretches credulity to the breaking point. A new parade of legal challenges will soon test the sincerity of the court on that; the stage has been set by the Ontario Court of Appeal's recent decision to "allow" a child to have three legal parents.[21] But the claim that the disagreement over the gender stipulation poses a problem only of degree – of a wider and a narrower view of marriage – is a still more obvious fiction. It serves the unstated purpose of situating the novel definition closer to the norm of natural law than the ancient one, thus turning the tables on the traditionalists, who seem to have confined marriage (for millennia!) within an artificial limit. Such a claim is self-defeating, of course, from the standpoint of natural law, but we needn't pursue that when outright incredulity is the sanest response. Does the court really expect us to believe that "the union of a man and a woman" or "the voluntary union of one man and one woman" were never anything more than narrow-minded variants of "the union of this person and that person"? That biology and reproduction were, so to say, Catholic or Puritan additions to the concept of marriage? Admittedly, it was in Christendom that the phrase "to the exclusion of all others" was inserted into the legal definition, establishing a chaste monogamy as the true norm of marriage and insinuating into the essence of marriage what, in other historic cultures and polities, has sometimes been regarded as inessential. The reasons for doing so were religious as well as sociological, and the court – given its inclination to oppose the civil to the religious – might reasonably have questioned *that*. Instead it questioned the phrase "one man and one woman" on the spurious grounds that this phrase meant nothing more than "two persons" all along. Who knew?

It is not the tradition but the court that has difficulty identifying "an objective core of meaning which defines what is 'natural' in relation to marriage." It is not the tradition but the court that is confused about whether a limit is natural or artificial. The consanguinity limit that states generally include in their regulatory apparatus is an example of an artificial limit, because it bears on the accidents of marriage rather than on its substance or nature. Not so with the gender stipulation, which is built right into the traditional definition and resides there even before the question of state regulation arises. The gender stipulation – or rather the gender-laden definition – indicates that marriage, whatever else it is, is naturally procreative and exists institutionally with a view to procreation and to the social conditions thereof. Otherwise the state would have no regulatory interest in the accidents of marriage, such as the degree of consanguinity or the minimum age of suitability or the number of marriages into which one might enter simultaneously.

In *Divorcing Marriage* I criticized the provincial courts for finding that the common-law definition of marriage is wrongfully discriminatory, when in fact it is only retroactively – after marriage has already been changed from an opposite-sex institution oriented to the bearing and raising of children to a mere partnership of sexual intimates – that the gender stipulation it contains could possibly be deemed discriminatory. Their argument, I observed, was not so much tautological as viciously circular.[22] If marriage were merely a publicly recognized close personal relationship between two adults, then an argument might be made (as per *Halpern*) that it violates equality rights to insist arbitrarily that the adults in question be of opposite sex. But if marriage is not that, if it is an institution aimed at the stable bonding of a father and a mother and their offspring – if it has three basic goods rather than just one or two – then the gender stipulation is anything but arbitrary and an equality rights case must fail. Recognizing this weakness, perhaps, the Supreme Court of Canada quietly tried to repair the argument by asserting that marriage has always been, at its core, a gender-blind construct to which *proles* is inessential;[23] but in so doing it only compounded the intellectual dishonesty of its provincial counterparts, for there can be no reconciliation between the old gender-laden definition and the new gender-neutral definition.

Enough, however, about our courts. The first condition of possibility for the state theft of marriage, or of the rights associated with marriage, is not the clumsy justification of the deed by those who wear the ermine. It is the people's own tendency in recent decades to divorce marriage, in practice if not in principle, from its intrinsic goods, and to seek gratification without renunciation. As one caller to a radio show on which I was a guest put it, we need C-38 and gay marriage "because everyone has the right to be happy." Neither our courts nor other branches of our rights industry have ventured quite that far into the realm of fancy, but the comment shows how much licence we have given them to do so. Ours is a generation on which the wisdom of the ages is lost, or from which it has been hidden. It is a pampered and perverse generation that supposes that everyone has a right to be happy. Whether or not the gods themselves be happy, happiness is not what Modestinus had in mind when he spoke of the divine and human rights that go with marriage. The rights that go with marriage, like the joys, are those that belong to the act of renunciation and to the responsibilities of the *proles, fides, et sacramentum.*

Bill C-38, to be fair, stops short of promising happiness, but not of formalizing our rejection of procreation as a defining good of marriage. It testifies to our abandonment of the other goods as well, and of our children's claim on the benefits that accrue through them. It makes official for all Canadians the end of marriage as the tie that binds parents to their children and children to their parents. Did we really mean to do that?[24] Have we understood the consequences? Marriage will no longer mark the transition "from the concerns of one generation towards a concern for the next." And if that transition is not to be marked by marriage, by what will it be marked? If effecting that transition is not the responsibility of those who marry, whose responsibility is it? Deprived of the recognition at law of our natural bonds, and of the rights and privileges they entail, we have become exposed in new and unnatural ways to the bonds of the state.[25]

III

Revolt Against the Family

The family may fairly be considered, one would think, an ultimate human institution. Every one would admit that it has been the main cell and central unity of almost all societies hitherto, except, indeed, such societies as Lacedaemon, which went in for "efficiency," and has, therefore, perished, and left not a trace behind. Christianity, even enormous as was its revolution, did not alter this ancient and savage sanctity; it merely reversed it. It did not deny the trinity of father, mother, and child. It merely read it backwards, making it run child, mother, father. This it called, not the family, but the Holy Family, for many things are made holy by being turned upside down. But some sages of our own decadence have made a serious attack on the family.

G. K. Chesterton[26]

IT was on 9 December 2004, one day prior to the celebration of Human Rights Day, that the court declared its support in principle for same-sex marriage and gave C-38 a green light. Writing in the *Globe and Mail* the day before the reference opinion came down, columnist John Ibbitson described the situation in terms of "a debate between Old Canada and New Canada," with their differing worldviews and ways of life, which had come to a head in the marriage issue.[27] Ibbitson was right, though his way of portraying the situation can certainly be faulted. Popular resistance to C-38, tangibly expressed the following spring by some 15,000 protestors from virtually every race and creed who gathered on Parliament Hill in the

March for Marriage and Freedom, demonstrated that it is not
(as he claimed) a matter of white, rural, religious Canada ver-
sus diverse, urban, agnostic Canada.[28] Nor is it the case that
Old Canada is failing while New Canada is advancing. New
Canada, as Mark Steyn tirelessly points out – if by "New
Canada" we mean, more honestly, the mainly white, agnostic
elite whose worldview was shaped back in the sixties and sev-
enties – may be trying hard to reproduce itself ideologically,
but is also trying hard *not* to reproduce itself biologically, and
for that reason alone (there are others, as we shall see) its claim
to the future must be questioned.[29] It may be agreed, however,
that the marriage issue belongs to a larger *Kulturkampf* and
that it is indeed a decisive battleground.[30]

This *Kulturkampf* began in earnest in the early decades of
the last century, with the promotion of sterilization, eugenics,
and the contraceptive mentality. It began, that is, as an attack
on children. The accompanying slaughter of the innocents,
which in the wake of C-150 quickly piled up the tiny mutilated
corpses – some 100,000 of them *per annum* – multiplied in our
collective conscience spot upon damned spot. No account of
same-sex marriage that ignores this prior defiling and sear-
ing of conscience can hope to be fully plausible, nor for that
matter any account that ignores the culture of divorce that also
emerged after C-150, scarring subsequent generations of living
children. This, however, is not the place to attempt a serious
description of such things, or to examine their own conditions
of possibility. It suffices to observe that same-sex marriage
has in reality nothing to do with the establishment of human
rights – if it did, the rights of children and parents would not
have been left out of the debate – and everything to do with a
revolt against the family. More specifically, it has to do with the

normalization of homosexuality, which is a signal, still largely subliminal, of society's rejection of the future that is opened up to it by the existence of the Holy Family.

It is futile to deny that the immediate purpose of same-sex marriage is the normalization of homosexuality. Things have come a long way since Harry Hay's quirky 1948 manifesto and the contentious days of the Mattachine Society. Things have come a long way since Stonewall, and even since Michael Swift's pungent attack just twenty years ago, in "The Gay Revolutionary," on what he called "the vicious heterosexual enemy."[31] Sanitizing and mainstreaming homosexuality is the prevailing political strategy. Those who are pursuing it have reason to be gay and a remarkable history of accomplishments of which to boast. In Canada and a handful of other countries, same-sex marriage is among them. If C-150 effected a transition from the criminalization of homosexual acts to their toleration, C-38 effected a transition from the toleration of homosexual acts to the celebration of homosexuality as such.[32] The celebration of homosexuality means that humanity is no longer merely male and female, but "heterosexual" and "homosexual." The institution by which this is recognized is not traditional marriage but same-sex marriage: marriage that, when performed, isolates rather than unites the sexes, but by its very existence as a legal regime enforces the political unity and social equality of heterosexuals and homosexuals. That is what is meant by normalization.

For some time it has been recognized among gay strategists that normalization is not so easy as erasing a page or two from the American Psychiatric Association's diagnostic manual and filling in the blank space with a newly discovered disorder called homophobia (a term re-minted for the culture wars by the Manhattan psychotherapist George Weinberg).[33] All such gains, vital as they are, are relativized, if not actually rebuffed, by marriage. Marriage is an institutional bulwark against the triumph of fornication in general and of homosexual relations in particular. To achieve the desired change in society's attitude to homosexuality, it has therefore been deemed necessary to overrun marriage and to introduce same-sex marriage. It has become obvious that equality-rights jurisprudence provides the best vehicle in which to do that, especially on Canadian terrain, and that embracing biological determinism (thus establishing a parallel with liberation and civil-rights movements) supplies the licence to drive.[34] Arguments about the dangers of the drive for same-sex marriage have been made, for normalization must exact its price, but the only real surprise has been the speed of which the vehicle has proved capable.

It is equally futile to deny that same-sex marriage is part and parcel of a revolt against the family. In Michelangelo Signorile's much-quoted words, first uttered more than a dozen years ago, the best plan "might be to fight for same-sex marriage and its benefits and then, once granted, [to] redefine the institution of marriage completely"; that is, "to demand the right to marry not as a way of adhering to society's moral codes, but rather to debunk a myth and radically alter an archaic institution that as it now stands keeps us down."[35] Signorile insisted that, as a matter of the highest priority, the very idea of the family must be transformed. This is being undertaken today in a variety of ways, whether through the soft-sell "menu approach" of William Eskridge and Darren Spedale in their recent book *Gay Marriage*, or through the sterner stuff on offer in dedicated gay venues like *Out* magazine, or through actions such as that of the Ontario Court of Appeal in the three-parents case, which the court rightly described as "important and novel."[36] Paula

Ettelbrick (trampling unawares on Trudeau's dictum) famously reminded fellow activists in the legal sphere that "being queer is more than setting up house, sleeping with a person of the same gender, and seeking state approval for doing so ... Being queer means pushing the parameters of sex, sexuality, and family, and in the process, transforming the very fabric of society ... We must keep our eyes on the goal ... of radically reordering society's view of reality."[37]

That goal is an old and familiar one. Hay and his early west coast comrades in the Mattachine Foundation were members of the Communist Party and, in addition to their own homosexual agenda, they shared the Marxist view of the bourgeois family, viz., that it could and should be abolished.[38] While same-sex marriage proponents have frequently dissociated themselves from this view for tactical reasons – they don't talk much about Hay,[39] never mind Marx or Engels, though Foucault may crop up – it is now openly advocated by many feminist and gay leaders, including the sizeable collection of American scholars who signed the document "Beyond Same-Sex Marriage."[40] In more than a few universities and law schools, belief in the abolition of the traditional family is *de rigueur*. Much of what is said and done in support of abolition sits uneasily, of course, beside the biological determinism that the modern gay-rights movement touts. Can the demand for "recognition and respect for our chosen relationships in their many forms," not to speak of animus against the strictures of the traditional family, really be rooted in biology or justified by a biological argument? Only a fool would suppose so. But then it needn't be rooted in Marxism either, as Pope Leo made clear when Marxism was still young. Marxism is only one root, and neither the deepest nor the most pervasive.

The denial that same-sex marriage belongs to a revolt against the family is futile, but it is not uncommon. The editorial pages in Canada's newspapers, almost unanimously, have declared the marriage debate over and the fabric of society more or less untouched. In their muddle-headed sentimentalism it is as if no *Kulturkampf* ever existed, or as if it were all a kind of game, of no more importance, say, than the latest outing of the Maple Leafs – who, as it happens, have lent their logo (at a good price, one assumes) to the propaganda film *Breakfast with Scot*,[41] "a budding queen of an eleven year-old boy." This is not Bolshevism at work. It is not even Foucaultism at work. It is capitalism at work, reaping in its decadent phase what it sowed in the days of its ascetic youth, when for the sake of profit it learned to manipulate the family and to regard children as objects or even obstacles. It is what Chesterton called "the living exultant energy of the rich, resolved to enjoy themselves at last, with neither Popery nor Puritanism nor Socialism to hold them back." It is what Gandhi called "the strong wine of libertinism" that has intoxicated the West.[42]

Yet there is something more going on here than a decadent, libertine capitalism can account for, even one that is greedily trying to digest various indigestible bits of mutated Marxism. The dull-wittedness, the deliberate ignorance, the stubborn denial of obvious facts, the simplistic sloganeering – "fiscally conservative, socially liberal" comes to mind – these things can perhaps be explained in that way, whether found in the press gallery or on the floor of the House. But what has happened in the House, under a Conservative as well as under a Liberal government, must give us pause. Not three but four times, a bill whose sole purpose is to normalize homosexuality, a pretentious and dishonest bill that covers up its naked revolt against the family with no less than ten justifying "whereas" clauses[43] – surely something of a record – has passed muster. And no party leader has offered so much as a solid paragraph in defence of the rights of children and of parents on which that bill tramples. One might almost suppose that the legislative branch (which, as the Supreme Court pointed out in declining to answer the final reference question, did not even exhaust its legal options before bringing the bill forward) had its own reason for undermining the family; that in fact it welcomed the opportunity to break down this "ultimate human institution," one that serves to mediate between the individual and the state, buffering the former from the latter.[44]

The thought is a tempting one, but I am not about to offer a conspiracy theory in explanation of the "something more." Shall we speculate that Trudeau's heirs secretly willed the death of his dictum, or at least recognized that dictum to be incompatible with the statism he himself encouraged? Could they possibly have been clear-sighted enough to see that, in a society that owns no standard or ideal form either of sexual or of domestic relationships, all responsibility for the individual, particularly the vulnerable individual, passes over to the state? That same-sex marriage will therefore help to make the Canadian state more powerful – more invasive in the lives of its own citizens, that is – than anyone ever imagined?[45] To be frank, neither Trudeau nor his successors were capable of thinking on that level. If conspiracies there were, they were on the pettier level of the lobbyists and lawyers and their cabinet friends. A better explanation for the success of C-38 is that the House of Commons is suffering the same fate as that "ancient house of man," the family, which has been rotting away from the "worms of secret sensuality and individual appetite."[46]

Still, I do think there is something more at work here. I said earlier that the normalization of homosexuality is a signal of our rejection of the future that is opened up to us by the existence of the Holy Family. By that I meant that same-sex marriage speaks, if we are really listening, not of the glories of a free society, but of the pessimism and despair into which our self-indulgent culture is finally beginning to sink. Mary's *Fiat mihi secundum verbum tuum (Be it done unto me according to Thy word)*, and Joseph's taking of the pregnant Mary as his wife, stand in stark contrast to our post-Christian rejection of children as an expensive inconvenience, or even (when we wish to appear noble rather than selfish, while persuading others to behave no better than ourselves) as a threat to planetary welfare. Likewise, the gospel announced to Mary, with its "Fear not!", stands in the sharpest possible contrast to the hopelessness that has begun to characterize Western society.

Marriage is no longer about children! What state of mind, what condition of heart and soul, is necessary to say such a thing? Marriage itself has been sterilized. It is no longer about being a parent and a grandparent, or even an uncle or an aunt. It is not about making and sustaining families – families that lovingly include the infertile without loving infertility – with siblings, cousins, nephews, and nieces. Marriage is not about forming and maintaining the basic cells of civil society, the plenipotent cells that replenish society and fill it with the fruit of their diversity. Marriage, as made in Canada, is merely about coupling and copulation. To paraphrase Paula Ettelbrick, it is state-approved fornication: a temporary stop on the road to nowhere in particular.[47] That perhaps is all marriage *can* be, if it is not permitted to be a sign of hope for the future of the race; if indeed it is not permitted to be a step on the road to that eschatological future that Saint Paul had in mind, when, quoting the famous passage from Genesis – "For this cause shall a man leave his father and mother, and shall be joined unto his wife, and they two shall be one flesh" – he added, "This is a great mystery: but I speak concerning Christ and the church."[48]

The onset of depression is often marked by erratic behaviour before the depression itself is recognized or diagnosed. Bill C-38, the very thought of which was overwhelmingly rejected in the House as recently as 1999, is such a marker. I am inclined to conclude from its passage into law that Canadian society is entering into a serious depression, not of the economic variety – though that is a likely side effect of our thinning and graying population – but of the spiritual variety. There are very good reasons for this depression, to some of which I have already alluded. But fortunately there is also a cure. The revolt against the family, after all, though its victims (like King Herod's) are very real and all too numerous, is itself an exercise in futility. For the true subversion of the family took place two thousand years ago. It did not prevent a child but produced a child. And the child it produced is the Saviour, not only of the holy innocents, but, if they will have it, of guilty adults too. ▦

Notes

1   The *Buggery Act* was repealed in 1553, reinstated in 1563, and repealed again in 1828, though buggery remained illegal in Britain until 1967. More recently, the celebrated *Lawrence v. Texas* (2003) has dealt with some of the same issues, albeit in a rather altered context.

2   Bill S-10, *An Act to amend the Marriage (Prohibited Degrees) Act and the Interpretation Act in order to affirm the meaning of marriage*, was introduced in the Senate by Ann Cools and subsequently defeated. See Debates of the Senate (Hansard), 3rd session, 37th Parliament, 141, Issue 32, 22 April 2004.

3 See *Familiaris Consortio* (1981) §2.

4 It should not surprise anyone that a country that not only encourages but also enforces contraception, not stopping even at the unspeakable wickedness of forced abortions, is a country capable (or so we have heard recently) of forced organ donations. But it should be noted that the UN Population Fund is financially complicit in the former, implicating a host of other nations in the fulfillment of Pope Paul's grim predictions.

5 Decriminalization, after all, was mere toleration; and toleration, some were already proposing, should give way to the celebration of sexual diversity. The demand for same-sex marriage *is* the demand for celebration, and it will not stop with same-sex marriage (see below).

6 See again Debates of the Senate (Hansard), 3rd session, 37th Parliament, 141, Issue 32, 22 April 2004.

7 Cf. F. C. DeCoste, "Courting Leviathan: Limited Government and Social Freedom in Reference Re Same-Sex Marriage" (2005) 42 *Alberta Law Review* 1099-1122, sec. 2(d).

8 "Perversion: An 'Outdated' Concept, Desperately and Perpetually Needed," *National Review*, 14 June 2004 (available at http://www.highbeam.com/doc/1G1-130931687.html).

9 *Corpus Iuris Civilis: Digest* 23.2.1. Cf. Pius XI, *Casti Connubii* §9, §84 (1930).

10 Including our Supreme Court? Cf. *Reference re Same-Sex Marriage* (2004 SCC 79), §22.

11 Paul Martin Sr, House of Commons, Special Committee on Human Rights and Fundamental Freedoms, Minutes of Proceedings and Evidence, no. 10, 27 July 1960, 593. (I am indebted to Professor George Egerton for drawing my attention to this.)

12 Compare my remarks at the March for Marriage and Freedom, 9 April 2005, which may be heard here: http://www.catholic-legate.com/audio/farrow.mp3. See also "Why and How Canadians Should Refuse to Recognize C-38,"available at http://www.enshrinemarriage.ca/english/farrow0629.pdf.

13 Post-Christendom there may be no other way to re-sacralize the state – which Christianity de-sacralized with its eschatological concept of the *saeculum* – than for the state to expropriate marriage. Cf. Farrow, ed., *Recognizing Religion in a Secular Society* (McGill-Queen's, 2004), 157ff.

14 (2005) 42 *Alberta Law Review* 1099-1122.

15 I am aware that my language here will seem immoderate to many,
    unless perhaps they have read Rory Leishman's *Against Judicial
    Activism* or Robert Martin's *The Most Dangerous Branch*. But even
    those who resent this growing chorus of objections to the judiciary's
    abuse of the *Charter* may reasonably ask why the Supreme Court,
    in the issue at hand, did not match the honesty of Justice Robert
    Blair in the original *Halpern* decision, who pointed out that the
    "transformation in the concept of marriage" entailed by the new
    definition is not incremental but profound, and that it "is laden
    with social, political, cultural, emotional and legal ramifications"
    (see *Halpern* v. *Canada (A.G.)*, [2002] 60 O.R. (3d) 321 (Ont. Div. Ct.),
    para. 97ff.).

16 *Not* of homosexual individuals, please note, since marriage has
    always been among their options.

17 See "The War of the Ring," in Cere and Farrow, eds., *Divorcing
    Marriage* (McGill-Queen's, 2004), 11ff. See also Cere's report *The
    Future of Family Law* (Institute for American Values, 2005), 12ff.

18 To quote the authors of "Beyond Same-Sex Marriage: A New Strategic
    Vision for All Our Families and Relationships," 26 July 2006 (available
    at: http://www.beyondmarriage.org/full_statement.html). The
    range would be wide enough to include polyamorous relationships,
    for example, for which apologists are now quite plentiful.

19 *Reference re Same-Sex Marriage*, para. 27.

20 para. 28

21 *A.A.* v. *B.B.*, 2007 ONCA 2 [2 January 2007] C39998. Now that little
    Johnny can have three parents, would we not be discriminating
    against him if we didn't allow his parents to marry?

22 Marriage, it is said, is an intimate relationship between adults. Jill
    and Jane are intimate adults. Therefore Jill and Jane must be allowed
    to marry or their rights will be violated. And what prevents them
    from marrying? The common-law definition. Conclusion? We must
    change the definition. And to what will we change it? Well, to "a
    union of two persons" – that is, to an intimate relationship between
    adults. If the Supreme Court is looking for tautology, there it is!
    And if this dishonest argumentation, which takes its conclusion as a
    premise, is not acknowledged as such and rooted out, the integrity
    of the law will certainly be the next casualty of same-sex "marriage,"

after marriage itself and the mutual rights of children and parents. Equality-rights jurisprudence in particular will be set chasing its own tail, until it has devoured itself in a destructive frenzy. (Cf. *Divorcing Marriage*, 98f.)

23 I say "quietly" because the court refused to address the fourth reference question head on.

24 On the eve of the parliamentary vote that reconfirmed Bill C-38 (7 December 2006), an MBA research poll showed that an overwhelming majority of Canadians continue to believe in the right of children to be reared by both a father and a mother; yet the connection between this right and the definition of marriage seems to have evaded most Canadians and their parliamentary representatives.

25 Though writing in the American context, which is not yet quite so dire as the Canadian, Professor Stephen Baskerville nicely sizes up the situation: "Undermining traditional marriage threatens not only the family and social stability, but civil freedom ... Once marriage becomes detached from procreation ... the entire system of domestic and social stability that marriage exists to foster unravels. Marriage then is no longer an autonomous and self-renewing institution, mediating the generational interface between public and private, and therefore limiting government power. Instead, it becomes merely a prize in the competition for power and one to be passed out by the very state it once served to control, a form of government patronage handed out to favored groups based on their relative power, like jobs or contracts. That is precisely what has now happened" ("The Real Danger of Same-sex Marriage," *The Family in America*, vol. 20, nos. 5-6, May-June 2006; available at http://www.profam. org/pub/fia/fia.2005.6.htm).

26 *Brave New Family* (Ignatius, 1990), 37; from *Heretics*, in Collected Works, vol. 1.

27 "It's up to PM to Ensure Same-sex Bill Passes" (8 December 2004, A4).

28 The mainstream media decided, by and large, to pretend that this event, of 9 April 2005, had not happened. Some outlets that did report it falsely claimed that the crowd numbered around 4,000 – about 25% of its actual size. When Stephen Harper addressed the crowd briefly, his best line was, "Looks like Canada to me!" Once he was in power, however, it became apparent that his interest in the event was largely opportunistic.

29 Apropos here is the concluding line of Paul Bureau's *L'Indiscipline des Moeurs* (ET 1925: *Towards Moral Bankruptcy*), to which Gandhi draws our attention in his own rejection of the contraceptive mentality (Collected Works, vol. 36 [1926], 214): "The future is for the nations who are chaste." But this future, if it is to be at all, will have to be fought for.

30 Cf. "Culture Wars Are Killing Marriage," *National Post*, 7 May 2003, A18 (available at http://www.marriageinstitute.ca/pages/culwars.htm).

31 The combination of playfulness and earnestness in this possibly pseudonymous diatribe – which was published in 1987, the year the Mattachine Society finally folded due to infighting and impending bankruptcy – makes it a curious and bracing read. To dismiss it as pure self-satire is foolish, however, since its earnestness and indeed its prophetic power can hardly be denied. Its lynchpin line contains a psychologically profound and politically germane insight: "For us too much is never enough."

32 Gay activists have left us a solid paper trail setting out their ambitions. From *The Homosexual: Oppression and Liberation* (1971) by Dennis Altman, who carried the torch in academia following Stonewall, to *After the Ball* (1989) by Marshall Kirk and Hunter Madsen, who without embarrassment laid out their compulsory sex therapy for America, to Ian Macgillivray's *Sexual Orientation and School Policy* (2004), with its bold call for "restorative" if not punitive justice, they have been designing and promoting programs for broad social change leading from de-criminalization through toleration to celebration.

33 See "Sexual Politics and Language," *National Post*, 31 August 2001 (available at http://www.marriageinstitute.ca/pages/sexpol.htm).

34 The unsubstantiated claim that "sexual orientation" is biologically based, which should not be confused with speculation that homosexual tendencies may be biologically influenced, is tied to a particular political strategy. It has been used to extend Hay's effort to mimic the successes of African Americans – Hay was the first to propose that gays should also barter with politicians, exchanging votes for support – to the point of inserting the gay community into the righteous penumbra of the civil-rights movement. In its extended

form, the argument runs that politicians *ought* to support gays,
because gays are born gay; not to support them would be to deny
their human dignity. Hay himself did not like this strategy, however.
He understood homosexuality to be primarily a spiritual matter.

35 See "Bridal Wave,"*Out* (December 1993-January 1994), 161, and
"I Do, I Do, I Do, I Do, I Do," *Out* (May 1996), 30. "I have found a
gap" (para. 40).

36 Para. 41. Taking an expansive view "of the exercise of the *parens
patriae* jurisdiction" (para. 29), Rosenberg J.A. justifed the court's
decision in terms of the child's welfare. His comment at para. 35
reveals another motive, however – the same that was evident in
Halpern – namely, to push the parameters of the family: "Present
social conditions and attitudes have changed. Advances in our
appreciation of the value of other types of relationships and in
the science of reproductive technology have created gaps in the
[*Children's Law Reform Act*'s] legislative scheme. Because of
these changes the parents of a child can be two women or two men.
They are as much the child's parents as adopting parents or 'natural'
parents. The *CLRA*, however, does not recognize these forms of
parenting and thus the children of these relationships are deprived
of the equality of status that declarations of parentage provide."
The putative concern with the status of the child is merely a cover
for the concern to assign value to the relationship between the
lesbian couple and to their relationship with the sperm donor (who
is necessary in order to compensate for the natural infertility of a
lesbian relationship).

37 "Since When is Marriage a Path to Liberation?", in *Lesbians, Gay
Men, and the Law*, ed. W. Rubenstein (The New Press, 1993), 398ff.
My source for the quotations from Signorile and Ettelbrick is Glen
Lavy's "Behind the Rhetoric: The Social Goals of GLBT Advocacy in
Corporate America" (available at http://corporateresourcecouncil.
org/white_papers/Behind_The_Rhetoric.pdf). Lavy remarks (p. 3)
that "though Ettelbrick views marriage, no matter how broadly
defined, as a hindrance to her social goals, she supports the idea of
undermining traditional marriage by making it available to gays
and lesbians."

38 Besides *The Communist Manifesto*, see e.g. *The German Ideology*,
where we are told that we "cannot speak at all of the family 'as

such'" (180), and that we certainly must not absolutize the
"Christo-Teutonic" form of the family (Marx and Engels, Collected
Works, 1976; cf. Michael Banner, *Christian Ethics and Contemporary
Moral Problems*, Cambridge University Press, 1999, 226ff.).

39 Hay was not welcome in the New York Mattachine Society partly
because of his communism, though he was put out of the Communist
Party as well, partly because of his homosexual activism. Later on
his sturdy support for NAMBLA kept him on the sidelines of the
politically successful gay organizations, though at his death in 2002
he was hailed by all as a great pioneer.

40 See http://www.beyondmarriage.org/full_statement.html. Re:
Michel Foucault, see e.g. "Sexual Morality and the Law," chap. 16 in
his *Politics, Philosophy, Culture* (Routledge, 1988).

41 Adapted from Michael Downing's 1999 book of the same title.

42 More fully: "For the next great heresy is going to be simply an attack
on morality; and especially on sexual morality. And it is coming, not
from a few Socialists surviving from the Fabian Society, but from
the living exultant energy of the rich resolved to enjoy themselves
at last, with neither Popery nor Puritanism nor Socialism to hold
them back. The thin theory of Collectivism never had any real roots
in human nature; but the roots of the new heresy, God knows, are as
deep as nature itself, whose flower is the lust of the flesh and the lust
of the eye and the pride of life. I say that the man who cannot see this
cannot see the signs of the times; cannot see the sky signs in the street
that are the new sort of signs in heaven. The madness of to-morrow
is not in Moscow but much more in Manhattan ..." (*G.K.'s Weekly*,
19 June 1926; courtesy of Dale Ahlquist, president of the American
Chesterton Society). Gandhi's warning came in the same year: "Let
us beware of the strong wine of libertinism that the intoxicated West
sends us under the guise of new truth and so-called human freedom"
(Collected Works, vol. 36, 212).

43 For an analysis of these clauses, see my remarks to the Legislative
Committee on Bill C-38, Meeting 14 (38th Parliament, 1st Session),
7 June 2005 (available at http://www.marriageinstitute.ca/pages/
FARROWBRIEF.pdf).

44 Following Alexander Zinoviev, William Grigg points us to
the blueprint of the Italian communist Antonio Gramsci, who
"understood that the creation of the total state requires the

seizure of the 'mediating institutions' that insulate the individual from the power of the government – the family, organized religion, and so forth – and *a systematic* redefinition of the culture in order to sustain the new political order" (http://www.grecoreport.com/gramsci_a_method_to_the_madness.htm).

45 Here I want to stand Foucault on his head, though I doubt that that will make him holy. I also want to observe that such a society must have its own official moral diseases or thought-crimes; e.g., "homophobia" and "heterosexism." Overt manifestations of these diseases – anything that betrays the benighted view that homosexuality, as the Catholic Church puts it, is a disordered condition – are already punishable, as a growing number of Europeans and North Americans can attest.

46 Cf. Chesterton, *Brave New Family*, 192.

47 Is that not implied in always "pushing the parameters" of sex and the family? The conclusion to Tolkien's famous trilogy springs to mind, as the thesis to which Ettelbrick's vision is the antithesis: "But Sam turned to Bywater, and came up the Hill, as day was ending once more. And he went on, and there was yellow light, and fire within; and the evening meal was ready, and he was expected. And Rose drew him in, and set him in his chair, and put little Elanor upon his lap. He drew a deep breath. 'Well, I'm back,' he said."

48 Ephesians 5:31-32 (KJV). In other words, if marriage's deepest sacramental dimension is something to be feared, if its civil or secular nature must be carefully sealed off from its religious or eschatological potential, then even its temporal purpose may be negotiable. Marriage may be turned in on itself, so that it is no longer fecund even in the usual this-worldly sense.

On the Half-life
of Half-witted Legislation

Let's to these simple men; for many sweat

Under this act, that knows not the law's debt

Which hangs upon their lives; for silly men

Plod on they know not how, like a fool's pen,

That, ending, shows not any sentence writ,

Linked but to common reason or slightest wit:

These follow for no harm; but yet incur

Self penalty with those that raised this stir.

SIR THOMAS MORE, ACT II, SCENE III

Pundits and politicians convinced that the marriage debate is over took one in the eye when the Court of Appeal for Ontario (ONCA) handed down *A.A. v. B.B.* on 2 January 2007. It seems they got things exactly backwards after the parliamentary vote in Ottawa, a month earlier, that reaffirmed Bill C-38. It's not Bill C-38 that will endure and the marriage debate that will expire. It's C-38 that will expire and the marriage debate that will continue for the foreseeable future – until we are done with marriage itself.

The marriage debate hotted up about four years ago, when ONCA's famous *Halpern* ruling upheld a lower-court decision to strike the words "one man and one woman" from the definition of marriage and replace them with the words "two persons." It has received a new lease on life from ONCA's latest ruling, which overturned a lower-court decision and the limitation of legal parents to two. The new number for the moment is three, since ONCA thinks that little Johnny, to give D.D. a name, requires precisely three: his mother (C.C.); her lesbian partner (A.A.); and their male friend (B.B.), who made

An earlier version of this article appeared in the *Western Standard* under the title, "The Marriage Trap" (12 February 2007), shortly after *A.A. v. B.B.* was handed down. For the original contexts of the numerous quotations from *A.A. v. B.B.*, consult the judgment online at http://www.ontariocourts.on.ca/decisions/2007/january/2007ONCA0002.htm.

the donation that enabled them to start a family and who sees Johnny twice a week.

Many people worry, as the lower court worried, about the implications of this ruling for family law. If children can have more than two legal parents, just how many can they have, and on what basis? How will it be decided whether this or that person is involved in the child's life in such a way and to such a degree as to warrant the status of parent? What impact will it have on the child when multiple parents go multiple ways? How will custody cases be settled? These are good questions, as ONCA allows. Sooner or later the courts will have to generate the necessary principles and precedents for resolving them. But what's the connection with C-38 and the marriage debate?

At first glance the connection may seem tenuous, since *A.A.* v. *B.B.* does not deal with a marriage, is not a *Charter* case, and doesn't even mention *Halpern*. Still, there can be little doubt about its lineage. When in *Halpern* ONCA severed the relation between marriage and reproduction in order to extend marriage to same-sex couples, it also severed the relation between natural parenthood and legal parenthood. It could hardly do otherwise if it really intended to put same-sex couples on equal legal footing with opposite-sex couples. As the consequential amendments to C-38 make clear, legal parenthood now floats free of biological parenthood in a way that it has never done before. So where nature provides for only two parents, the law may, if it likes, provide for more. And in Ontario it has.

The connection goes deeper than that, however. At the heart of this ruling lies the *Children's Law Reform Act*, which sought to remove the disadvantages of children born outside of wedlock. In the spirit of that Act, ONCA has exercised "the court's inherent *parens patriae* jurisdiction" to prevent a child from being "deprived of the equality of status that declarations of parentage provide": in Johnny's case, "the legal recognition ... of one of his mothers." In doing so, it has further entrenched the self-defeating tendency of family law to undermine marriage, this time by overturning the two-parent norm that the institution of marriage embodies and upholds. I say "self-defeating" because there is overwhelming evidence that intact monogamous marriages are what children need and what a child-friendly state should be trying to encourage.

On a deeper level still, *A.A.* v. *B.B.* demonstrates what happens politically when a society marginalizes marriage or artificially restricts its mandate in the way that *Halpern* and C-38 have: the state's *parens patriae* power increases dramatically to fill the void. The burden of deciding what is good for a particular child – who shall be recognized as its parents, etc. – is no longer confined to exceptional cases. *A.A.* v. *B.B.* is in its way an exceptional case, to be sure; the court calls it "important and novel." But its importance and its novelty derive from the fact that its aim is to remove the norm by which exceptions might be measured. Exceptional situations, you see, must be rendered ordinary and unexceptionable, lest anyone suffer a dignity deficit. ONCA agrees and has disposed of the norm, leaving the court itself with unbridled power to determine who or what makes a parent.

It is evident, however, that ONCA has not yet bothered to think clearly about parenthood. The court states that A.A. seeks "legal recognition of her relationship with her son," who seems to be her son because she has been intimate with his mother for some time, intends him as her son, and finds him capable of using the word "momma" in a charmingly inclusive manner. ONCA is impressed by all of this. It grants the recognition

A.A. desires, but in its magnanimity does not strip B.B. of *his* recognition, which is based, rather more narrowly, on biology. The court hesitates only briefly over the fact that A.A. lacks any biological relation to Johnny – just long enough, in fact, to take a poke at the *Children's Law Reform Act*'s emphasis on natural parenthood by observing that "advances in reproductive technology require re-examination of the most basic questions of who is a biological mother." Certainly ONCA gives no hint that it knows how or when biology *is* relevant to parenthood, or why it deems it relevant in the case of B.B. and C.C., but not in the case of lesbian partner A.A.

Had the court been thinking clearly about parenthood, it would have begun with the natural mother, C.C., who is strangely absent here. C.C. is the key to this triangle, because she alone is connected to Johnny both by nature and by nurture. A.A. is connected by nurture, not nature; B.B. by nature, not nurture. Only with C.C. are we still in touch with the classical model of parenthood, in other words, and so also with the family law tradition. What is unusual about C.C., where she differs from the classical model, is that her partner in nature, B.B., is not her partner in nurture, which is A.A. Such are the basic facts from which the court should have reasoned.

Now when we approach the problem in this way, what stands out is not C.C.'s lesbianism, and not our growing prowess at medicalized sex – the novelties that allowed ONCA to posit a gap in the old legislation through which it could drive its three-parent decision. What stands out, rather, is what C.C. has in common with any woman who has borne the child of one man but decided (for reasons good or bad) to raise it with another. What the law always did with such cases, for the sake of the child, was force the adults to make a choice, in hopes of preserving as far as possible something analogous to the natural relationship. Three parents was never an option.

ONCA never faces this issue directly. "I have found a gap," declares Justice Rosenberg triumphantly, but his gap is nothing but a blind alley. What makes this ruling so abominable, however, is not the deliberate looseness of its reasoning but the court's lack of seriousness about what makes for the good parenting of children. The ease with which it dismisses centuries of wisdom on that topic, even while assuming astonishing new powers to define parenthood, betrays its bad faith. Indeed, this ruling is not really about parenthood at all, much less what's good for Johnny. Like *Halpern*, it is about "advances in our appreciation of the value of other types of relationships" than the kind championed by traditional marriage.

Our pundits and politicians, I realize, are politely stifling yawns. This kind of debate can go on forever without worrying folk who desire nothing more than the pottage of political compromise and the approving pats of the progressive-minded. It sounds like C-38 is quite safe after all. But the more astute among them will realize that ONCA has just put a spike through the heart of the prime minister's strategy on same-sex marriage. Poor Stephen Harper! Poor Bill C-38, demanded by ONCA in 2003, passed with great travail in 2005, and reaffirmed to widespread relief in 2006! How long will it last once little Johnny discovers from his lawyers (shall we call them E.E. and F.F.?) that C-38 won't allow his three legal parents to marry each other?

Bill C-38, you see, has a planned obsolescence. It has a built-in dignity-deficit trigger. There can be only one solution to the harm that it is about to do to Johnny's newly acquired sense of self-worth. Someone will have to pluck up the courage (I'm sure

ONCA will help with that if necessary) to introduce a new bill dropping the "two" from "union of two persons." Only then will little Johnny be free from C-38's sting of exclusion. When the new bill is passed, of course, it may be more difficult to say just what a union of persons is for. But under C-38 it's already impossible to say that it's for raising little Johnny, so a new bill there will have to be. C-38, R.I.P. ▦

Nation of Bastards

Musings on Marriage and Freedom

Marriage, for instance, being a civil contract, has civil consequences; and without them it is impossible for society even to subsist. If we assume that the clergy succeed in arrogating to themselves the sole right to perform the act of marriage, a right which, of necessity, they will usurp whenever they serve an intolerant religion, is it not obvious that, by establishing the authority of the Church in this matter, they will render that of the Prince null, and create a situation in which the Prince will have as subjects only such as the clergy shall see fit to give him? Being in a position to permit or to refuse marriage, according as whether those concerned do, or do not, hold certain doctrines, whether they admit or denounce the validity of this or that formula, whether they be more or less devout, the Church, surely, if only it use a little tact and refuse to yield ground, will be the sole controller of inheritances, offices, citizens, and the State itself, which could not continue were it composed only of bastards.

J.-J. ROUSSEAU, *THE SOCIAL CONTRACT* IV.8

I believe that the phrase "nation of bastards" entered common parlance via an article by Max O'Rell in the *North American Review* (March 1895), entitled "Mark Twain and Paul Bourget," with O'Rell – or so Twain suggests – acting as amanuensis to Bourget, who accused Twain of having launched that barb at France. Twain denied having used the phrase, reminding Bourget that the target of his gibe had been the French aristocracy. A century later the phrase became a notorious headline in the *Sydney Daily Telegraph*, which ran on 23 September 1997 over an article that pointed out that some thirty per cent of Australian children were being born out of wedlock. The headline was painful in a country in which the phrase already had a history, given Australia's colonial background. Where I live, of course, that same statistic would be sensational for another reason. For in New France (a land with a sensitive history of its own, coloured by a rare combination of resentments: both of the British crown and of the Catholic Church) the figure is now nearly double that, some fifty-nine per cent of children being born out of wedlock. Whatever the truth about Australia, Quebec is indeed en route to becoming a nation of bastards, and the rest of Canada is not so very far behind.

Well, what of it? Do such developments really threaten our social or political integrity? Do they put in doubt the future of the state? I want to attend here, with Rousseau, to marriage as a public institution; that is, to marriage as a civil contract with civil consequences. Only I will not assume that the state could not continue were it composed only of bastards.[1] I want rather to suggest that a state composed only of bastards might be the ideal state for which Rousseau is looking. (At all events, the immediate danger to the state today is not the high percentage of bastards but the fact that a dramatic decline in the birth rate means that soon there will not be enough bastards to go around.) I will not assume, either, that marriage is merely a civil contract. If marriage is in fact to have any future as a public institution, it will require a richer conceptual framework than the notion of a civil contract provides. It will require something even more than a preference for the older Lockean liberalism over the early Rawlsian approach that is presently in the ascendancy. It will require a public rehabilitation of the notion of covenant, the decline of which John Witte has documented in the final chapters of *From Sacrament to Contract*.[2]

My concern here is not directly with the distinction between covenant and contract, however. It is with the relation between marriage and political freedom, and so also between marriage and religion; for there is no such thing as a non-religious basis for freedom. I want to contend that marriage, understood in classical Christian terms, is a bulwark of human freedom within the state and, if need be, over against it. From that perspective a nation of bastards (even in sufficient supply) is indeed a problem, to which marriage can only be the solution if its covenantal character, the character lent to it by religion, is publicly recognized and widely coveted. If coveted, also respected, I may add. The bastards of the French aristocracy, after all – hence Twain's gibe – were as likely to be born to a married as to an unmarried mother. And, to paraphrase Andrew Sullivan, we are all aristocrats now.

Divide and Conquer

Rousseau's footnote on marriage in *The Social Contract* illustrates his concern that theological intolerance (he has Catholicism in view, of course) cannot but have a detrimental effect on civil life. He was prescient in singling out marriage as an important battleground. His proposal, which was taken up in the revolution, was to wrest marriage from the church and make it a civil affair under state control. In France today civil marriage precedes, and must precede, religious marriage, which is said to be something different. In North America a similar battle over marriage is now being fought, a strategic battle to divide civil from religious marriage, as part of a larger struggle to overcome the detrimental effects of theological intolerance. Remove religiously motivated restrictions on marriage and it is much easier to remove religiously motivated restrictions on human behaviour generally, and on the state's power to order human society as it sees fit.

As a footnote to his footnote, it may be recalled that Rousseau had a certain personal antipathy to marriage that went beyond the fact that marriages were liable to produce children, who can be frightfully inconvenient when trying to write books or otherwise impress high society. (He put his own children in an orphanage, as everyone knows, thanks to Voltaire.) Rousseau equated liberty with autonomy, and autonomy, he believed, was badly compromised not only by children but by the many religious and social conventions woven into marriage. In seeking relief from these, he looked to the state. Loyalty to the state could be used to trump those other claims of allegiance that had a nasty habit of inhibiting the autonomous ego. That said, the main justification he offered for state control of marriage was that marriage is a civil contract with civil consequences. It has an impact at once economic (transmission of wealth), social (standing and influence in civil society), and political (the rearing of new citizens). As a civil contract with civil consequences, its validation ought to lie in the gift of the state rather than of the church, lest through it the church achieve control of the state by allowing the latter only such subjects as the church already holds in liege.

It is not common at the moment to identify the struggle over marriage in these terms, though some Canadians come close to doing so (gay activists such as Kevin Bourassa and Joe Varnell, for example, or lesbian lawyer Barbara Findlay). Deceptive and misleading terms, borrowed from a shared human-rights discourse, are generally preferred. But in Canada we have been developing a distinction between civil and religious marriage that follows the French model. Bill C-38 speaks only of "marriage for civil purposes" and says nothing directly about religious marriage. In its reference opinion, however, the Supreme Court of Canada spoke of civil marriage and religious marriage as if they referred to two different things, rather than to two different ways of enacting the same thing. In subsequent public debate it has often been maintained, on just that assumption, that what is done to the one need not affect the other. Thus is it pretended (as also in the preamble and in section three of C-38) that a political controversy over religion can be avoided.

This facile distinction between civil and religious marriage – facile because, as Ted DeCoste points out,[3] the court nowhere defines it – makes it easier for the state to assume full control over marriage as a public institution. It reinforces the false notion that religion is essentially a private matter.[4] It also allows the state to claim that it is not really taking anything away from religion. From which it follows both that religious marriage can have no public significance and that civil marriage need not concern itself with any religious truth, even with the truth of natural law. Which is to say, the state is free to reinvent marriage as and when it pleases, along lines of its own choosing. That is the opinion of Canada's highest court.

The court supports itself by quoting the common-law definition of marriage provided by Lord Penzance in *Hyde* v. *Hyde*:

> What, then, is the nature of this institution as understood in Christendom? Its incidents may vary in different countries, but what are its essential elements and invariable features? If it be of common acceptance and existence, it must need (however varied in different countries in its minor incidents) have some pervading identity in a universal basis. I conceive that marriage, as understood in Christendom, may for this purpose be defined as the voluntary union for life of one man and one woman, to the exclusion of all others.[5]

"The reference to 'Christendom' is telling," comments the court. "*Hyde* spoke to a society of shared social values where marriage and religion were thought to be inseparable. This is no longer the case. Canada is a pluralistic society. Marriage, from the perspective of the state, is a civil institution."[6] It cannot escape legislative redefinition on the grounds that it has existed "in its present basic form since time immemorial" and is therefore "not a legal construct, but rather a supra-legal construct subject to legal incidents."[7]

Canada's highest judges have thus put their initials beside Rousseau's footnote.[8] For them the traditional heterosexual stipulation represents a past civilization in which religion had some purchase on the underlying foundations of social institutions such as marriage. That civilization, they say, no longer exists in Canada. The court stopped just short of saying that the new civilization, the *Charter* civilization, cannot countenance the heterosexual stipulation. But it did not stop short of pronouncing the liberation of civil society and of the state from all constraints of religion. Civil marriage is one thing, religious marriage another; they need share no common foundation and the latter has no bearing on the former. How far the former will nevertheless have a bearing on the latter, or at least on institutions that uphold the latter, remains to be seen, as the court admitted.

It may be observed in passing that the Supreme Court, in dismissing religion, did not altogether dismiss the notion of natural limits as a constraining factor in the definition of civil marriage. But leaning on a faulty analogy (the 1930 "Persons" case)[9] and on an even faultier analytical logic – as if "a union of two persons" were conceptually prior to "the union of a man and a woman" and not a mere abstraction from it – the court postulated a consensus about the objective core of marriage that does not exist.[10] And in doing so it failed to recognize that this supposed consensus actually robs marriage of its civil consequences.

Herein lies a great irony. By upholding the state's right to change the definition of marriage, on the grounds that the institution in question is strictly a civil contract with civil consequences, the court permitted and even encouraged the state to adopt a definition on which the institution has no civil consequences. No civil consequences, that is, except the one dearest to Rousseau: the liberation of the citizenry and of the state from the claims and influence of the church.

I overstate the case, some will say. But is it still necessary to explain that genderless marriage is incapable of the civil consequences for which marriage has chiefly been prized? What civil consequences has marriage when children are removed formally, legally, institutionally from its purview? Neither the items in Rousseau's list, nor those in any longer list of consequences that are plainly civil, make sense without the presupposition that marriages produce children and that the successful rearing of those children is largely, though not exclusively, what they are for. Genderless marriage is marriage in which procreation, *per definitionem*, is not the norm. The norm in genderless marriage is sexual bonding for its own sake, and its only immediate civil consequence is the normalization of homosexual bonding in the face of social resistance, especially religious resistance. Barbara Findlay was not mistaken when she insisted, nearly a decade ago, that "the legal struggle for queer rights will one day be a showdown between freedom of religion [and] sexual orientation."[11]

It will not do here to be too narrow, however. The success of the drive for genderless marriage is dependent on heterosexual interests as much as on homosexual interests. Marriage is a discipline that sets itself *inter alia* against the sexual proclivities of all men and women, whatever their sexual orientation or appetite. That is the moment of truth in Jonathan Rauch's claim that genderless marriage will do us all good by extending the domain of marriage into the homosexual community. If we could agree that marriage is not about approving either homosexuality or heterosexuality, but about chastity and faithfulness – that the goal of the new definition is nothing less than sexual discipline among homosexuals, a saving discipline that will make heterosexuals covet once again the grace of their religious birthright, so to speak, thus reforming a corrupt and immoral society – well, then, perhaps there might be something to talk about. But this is madness. Who really supposes that we are ready for this reform? Certainly no one imagines that we are changing the definition for this purpose. No one pretends that we are about to embark on some general program to discourage sex outside of marriage.

And why should we? Religion, remember, has lost its grip on us and may – nay, must – be discounted. Even children, for whose benefit this adult discipline is chiefly intended, no longer interest us in the same way they used to. That there are side benefits for adults from marriage is true enough: lower disease rates, longer life expectancy, a more stable community, a more stable economy, etc. But these benefits do not seem sufficiently compelling, or, if they do, we seek other means of achieving them.

Stephanie Coontz, for one, seems to think that we have already found most of what we need. Marriage, she contends, is no longer vital to modern societies and complaints about the collapse of the family are so much wasted energy. A global upheaval "has transformed the way people conduct their personal lives as thoroughly and permanently as the Industrial Revolution transformed working lives 200 years ago." Marriage just isn't the way we get things done any more. We have other ways of organizing our daily lives and labours, of looking after ourselves on the practical level. That is why marriage has become mainly a romantic institution and, as such, an inherently unstable one. "The origins of modern marital instability lie largely in the triumph of what many people [falsely] believe to be marriage's traditional role – providing love, intimacy, fidelity and mutual fulfillment. The truth is that for centuries, marriage was stable precisely because it was not expected to provide such benefits." Now that love is in the driver's seat, neither universality nor permanency is a feature we should expect to find in the institution.

According to Coontz, we must face up to the fact that marriage is not what it once was; it has changed irrevocably. "Marriage is no longer the institution where people are initiated into sex. It no longer determines the work men and women do on the job or at home, regulates who has children and who doesn't, or coordinates care-giving for the ill or the aged. For better or worse, marriage has been displaced from its pivotal position in personal and social life, and it will not regain it short of a Taliban-like counterrevolution." So then: "Forget the fantasy of solving the challenges of modern personal life by reinstitutionalizing marriage ... We cannot afford to construct our social policies, our advice to our own children and even our own emotional expectations around the illusion that all commitments, sexual activities and care-giving will take place in a traditional marriage."[12]

What's wrong with this picture, or is it essentially right? The basic idea seems to be that marriage, as a pre-romantic and pre-industrial public institution, was quite serviceable. It had useful civil consequences. But as a post-industrial institution it is useful chiefly for private romantic purposes. Which is to say, it is not really a public institution at all any more, or soon won't be. We are ready to move beyond conjugality, beyond marriage. If we discount traditional moral teaching as a prop to pre-industrial society, and overlook a few inconvenient facts, this appears to make sense – so long as we also admit that marriage isn't really about children, and that children don't really need, or especially benefit from, parents who marry and remain married.[13]

I wonder what Rousseau would say. He himself was no stranger to alternative arrangements. His mother died in child-birth and his father eventually abandoned him, but he landed on his feet and, aided by the church, got a good education. On the sexual side of life, after drifting from mistress to mistress, he found Thérèse, whom he did not marry but with whom he had several children (the same who made those one-way trips with him to the local foundling asylum, where few could hope to land on their feet). For all that, I think he would be bemused by Coontz-like denials that marriage is bound up with pro-creation and child-rearing, or that healthy child-rearing is bound up with marriage. But Rousseau is more than a little responsible for our present confusion. For he taught us to think about marriage, as I suspect Coontz does, in terms of a tension between an elusive fusion of egos (the romantic ideal) and the need to preserve personal autonomy in the face of enslaving social conventions. For Coontz, of course, marriage has lost much of its capacity to enslave because (like religion) it is no longer needed for the successful organization of human life. For the same reason it has lost much of its attraction, though some still find it convenient or romantically inspiring. On her view one can afford to be indifferent about same-sex marriage; there is no reason not to legalize it, for the simple reason that marriage itself hardly matters. Marriage now fails Rousseau's own test, the "civil consequences" test.[14]

But let us return to the point about religion. Rousseau also taught us this: to think of the state, not the church, as the conscience or transcending limit of marriage. Here his thought differs from Anglo-American contractarianism, which is libertarian in nature; yet the distance between Rousseau and J. S. Mill, say, is not very great. It would be quite possible, I think, to read the debates about marriage from Mill to the present moment in terms of a convergence between individualism and statism, both of which are marshalled against the church and its covenantal understanding of the foundations of human community – an understanding that does *not* equate freedom with autonomy, and that runs contrary to the contractarian myth about the so-called state of nature, the myth that underlies both individualism and statism in their modern forms.

Witte's conclusion in *From Sacrament to Contract* suggests that individualism is the great threat: "The elementary deconstructions and dismissals of a millennium-long tradition of marriage and family law and life seem altogether too glib to be taken so seriously. Yet the legal revolution marches on. And the massive social, psychological, and spiritual costs continue to mount up. The wild oats sown in the course of the American sexual revolution have brought forth such a great forest of tangled structural, moral, and intellectual thorns that we seem almost powerless to cut it down. We seem to be living out the grim prophecy that Friedrich Nietzsche offered a century ago: that in the course of the twentieth century, 'the family will be slowly ground into a random collection of individuals,' haphazardly bound together 'in the common pursuit of selfish ends' – and in the common rejection of the structures and strictures of family, church, state, and civil society."[15]

In "Courting Leviathan," on the other hand, Ted DeCoste is certain that statism is the great threat, especially in Canada. By means of its false distinction between religious and civil marriage, a distinction by which it supplants and ignores the distinction to which it ought to have attended – between the state and society – the Supreme Court has licensed the state to take possession of marriage in a paternalistic manner.[16] The state thus "commits itself to a redemptive politics that, by means and medium both, makes jest of limited government."

> Redemptive politics is a politics of conviction. The redemptive state is a state convinced that its proper purpose is to improve its subjects by imprinting on them, on their projects and character, the values that the state has made its own and declared superior. Such a state is not merely a custodian and guardian of the people's proper values, though it is clearly both. The redemptive state, rather, conceives of itself as the personification of those values and, with that, of the lives of the governed properly lived. Which is to say, state and people are, in theory, one, and so do they in fact become to the extent that the state succeeds in disarming the people of values that contradict or diminish its values. But this transformation, of the state into a person and persons into expressions of the state, comes at the cost, in equal measure, of moral arrogance by the state and of the moral disablement of the people.[17]

DeCoste concludes "that the Court has elevated politics over social life so as, first, to demand the conversion of the practitioners of faith and marriage to state values and, second, to weaken their fidelity to the life-world."[18]

I think that DeCoste's concern is now the more pressing one. In Canada, at least, the state has assumed the very position the church was once accused (as by Mill and Rousseau) of assuming: a position of dominance over civil society and the family and the individual. The *pater politicus* has sublated the *pater familias* as well as the *pater ecclesiasticus,* and marriage law is one means it has used. The grinding down of the family is not merely the result of opting for a contractarian model but of inviting the state to take control of marriage in the name of individual freedom.[19] Freedom, of course, is just what is being lost, as the neo-liberal state evolves its tyrannical power by hollowing out a place for itself inside the husk of human-rights discourse. The advent of same-sex marriage, trumpeted as a great triumph of human rights, marks an important milestone on the path to state tyranny.[20] For same-sex marriage makes bastards of us all, and as a nation of bastards we are all wards of the state.

How so? The change in definition uncouples marriage from procreation. From now on, then, no one will be born a bastard and everyone will be born a bastard. From now on, the connection between biological parenthood and legal parenthood will be supported by no institution. The claims of blood will not have the same standing at law that they once did. Natural relationships will not be primary at law; legal constructs will take their place, as they do in the consequential amendments of Bill C-38. Everyone, for legal purposes, will be first of all a ward of the state, and the state will become our primary community, as Rousseau intended it to.

Who Owns the Children?

Rousseau defended his actions in handing his own children over to the state by appealing to Plato's *Republic*. The Marquis de Sade seconded that appeal. Canada, as William Gairdner has pointed out, has its own share of those who claim that children belong ultimately to the state. He quotes, for example, the former chairman of Calgary's Board of Education, who advised parents in 1991: "The child is not your child, [children] are the property of the state, like our oil ..."[21] The case of those who advocate state ownership of children will only get stronger as the birthrate drops and this most precious commodity becomes more scarce. The need to educate children according to state values will thus become more pressing. No doubt it will prove to be in everyone's best interests if they are sometimes liberated from lesser (that is, familial) communities of concern, whose contractual powers will not extend so far. *Pater politicus* will see to the welfare of our potential contractors, while they remain underaged.

New illustrations of this kind of thinking present themselves on a daily basis. Take, for example, the recent decision of the European Court of Human Rights to uphold Germany's ban on home-schooling, a ban introduced under Hitler in 1938 and enforced last year, in one instance, by bursting into a home at night and hauling a mother of twelve off to prison.[22] The *European Convention on Human Rights* (Protocol No. 1, Article 2) states that "in the exercise of any functions which it assumes in relation to education and to teaching, the State shall respect the right of parents to ensure such education and teaching is in conformity with their own religious and philosophical convictions." Neither the German courts nor the European court, however, think too highly of this right. Parents, ruled the latter in the *Konrad* case, may not "on the basis of their convictions" refuse the right of a child to education – meaning the right to a state-controlled education.[23] The strategy here is a simple one: set children's rights in opposition to parental rights and interpose the state as arbiter of the putative conflict. Even if "it cannot be formally said that the applicant parents are seeking to impose their religious convictions against their children's will," insisted the court, the children "were unable to foresee the consequences of their parents' decision for home education because of their young age." The German courts were upheld in their finding that parents have no right to deprive their children of an education by the state and in accordance with the state's values. They were also supported in their claim that it is in "the general interest of society to avoid the emergence of parallel societies based on separate philosophical convictions and [to integrate] minorities into society."[24]

Here in Canada we might at least take exception to this last statement. Are we not (with apologies to Gilbert and Sullivan) the very model of the modern multicultural? Yet the two hands of the Canadian state, the judicial and the legislative, have for some decades been busy dismantling the natural family unit, on which authentic cultures depend. What a bundle of contradictions we are! Catholic prime ministers who support divorce, abortion, sperm banks, same-sex marriage. A Jewish justice minister who arranges that the words "natural parent" should be struck from Canadian law – surely one of the queerer signs of our queer times. And in Quebec the sovereigntist party, still reeling from its narrow but decisive referendum defeat by the more fertile "ethnic vote," subsequently elects as leader an icon of its own demographic impotence.

But where was I? While it is not yet illegal in Canada to home-school your children, it is fast becoming illegal to teach them anything by way of "separate philosophical convictions." Recent proposals in Europe and Britain to impose compulsory early childhood education, including sex education, are being mooted here as well. The "ideology of the family," as some now label it, is being rejected in favour of "deep changes in society in general and the family's structure in particular." There is a "paradigm shift from an exclusively family responsibility to a shared responsibility, which is the legitimation of out-of-home child socialization," entailing "a redefinition of public (state) and private (family) relationships concerning children's affairs" and "the recognition of the child's right to be cared for and socialized in a wider social context than that of the family."[25] In point of fact, family opt-out provisions respecting controversial subjects such as homosexual education are already being scrapped in public schools across the country; meanwhile, in a bizarre scenario in British Columbia, a naturally childless couple, Peter and Murray Corren, are busy rewriting the provincial social justice curriculum to make certain that everyone else's children are taught to think like they do.

Equally worrying is the paradigm shift that seems to be taking place in the thinking of our chief justice, Beverley McLachlin. In 1991, before attaining to that office, she delivered in Cambridge a paper entitled "Who Owns Our Kids? Education, Health and Religion in a Multicultural Society." Her intention was to contribute to the debate about when the state might "legitimately interfere ... with parental control of children." Her conclusion was a fairly guarded one, but tended in the opposite direction to that of the Calgary Board of Education chairman mentioned earlier. Recognizing that "religion cannot be divorced from how a family functions and children are reared," that "parents have the responsibility and consequently the right to deal with their children in accordance with their religious beliefs," and that any legal analysis "must start from the principle of parental autonomy," she was quite sympathetic to the view that "all reasonable presumptions should be made in favour of parental autonomy and family privacy." Courts, she said, "must guard against substituting their views of religion and morality for those of parents simply because the latter are different."[26]

In 2004, however, our chief justice revisited the topic in the Netherlands at the World Conference on Religion and

Education. There she emphasized much more strongly that rec-
onciling the free exercise of religion "with state objectives such
as the education of children" is no easy task. This is a paper of
questions, not of answers, but it evinces a degree of suspicion
of religion and of the family. Of one thing the chief justice is
certain, however: "In a diverse, multicultural world, tolerance
is the most important value. Whatever else we teach our children, we must teach them tolerance ... The rearing of children is
... the most profound responsibility that lies on any society. But
whatever our history, whatever our belief, we should always
remember that this is a responsibility, not a right. Too often in
the past, the welfare of children has been sacrificed to other
interests; too easily it has been relinquished in favour of more
compelling competing values. Too often religion has been used
not to make our children strong and free but rather to suppress
and stifle; not to make them tolerant, but rather to teach them
hate; not to incline them to peace, but rather to strife. Religion
is a fundamental element of our humanity. As such, it properly
occupies a central place in the rearing of our children ... [But
we] must teach them not only religion but above all, tolerance,
for surely that is what is in their best interests."[27]

If the rearing of children is any society's most profound
responsibility, our dramatically declining birthrate deserves a
notice she doesn't give it; that need not distract us from the
valid point she is making, however. Yet we may wonder what
answer this "tolerance *über Alles*" principle supplies to the
underlying dilemma about the relation between a family-based
culture of religious freedom and a school-based culture governed by the educational objectives of the state. The school, we
are now told, "is the primary environment for the socialization
of children, and for the construction of their identity," while tol-

erance is the "overarching virtue" that the schools must teach.[28] Does this not suggest that the family will have to take a back seat to the state, and "the historic imperative of religion" to "the modern imperative of tolerance"? McLachlin still thinks that the law can successfully mediate between these, but one may be forgiven for having doubts. Perhaps the question as to who owns the children was not the right question in the first place, if "parents and society are but children's guardians,"[29] but it is plain enough that the *parens patriae* looms larger in her thinking today than it did in 1991.[30]

Leaving the chief justice behind, permit me to pass for a moment from doubt to cynicism. Can the unprecedented changes and reversals we have witnessed in the last few years, as respects family law, be explained without positing a certain convergence of interests between the state and the so-called gay community when it comes to suppression of the natural family unit? To uphold the rights and interests of the natural family unit, as Article 16 of the *Universal Declaration of Human Rights* requires, is not, it seems, in the interests of either. It is not in the interests of the latter because homosexual couplings do not produce children and therefore cannot compete educationally without the coercive power of the state. It is not in the interests of the former because the natural family unit confronts the state internally, as another state confronts it externally, as a limiting factor. That this limiting factor makes for *freedom*, particularly when it is informed by Judeo-Christian convictions about modesty – not merely sexual modesty but political modesty, the modesty of the state – is of course denied. Family and church are denounced in Rousseauvian and indeed Marxist fashion as instruments of oppression. But who is making these denunciations? The very same, one is tempted to reply, who do not think it strange that a plainclothes policewoman should knock on the door of a tired *Hausfrau* late at night, with armed colleagues hiding in the bushes ready to burst in and make the arrest.

Perhaps such arrests will soon be unnecessary, given that modern reproductive technology and advances in bioethics are bringing the brave new world beyond conjugality ever closer to the opening scene of Huxley's famous novel.[31] Canada's *Civil Marriage Act*, which through its highly consequential amendments makes us all wards of the state, represents a crucial step in that direction, though even the Conservative Party will not publicly admit it.[32] When the state has finished using marriage to dismantle civil freedoms, it will, I predict, discard it altogether, much as Belinda Stronach discarded the Conservative Party. And unless I miss my guess, it will then turn its attention more directly to the problem of religion and in particular of the Catholic Church. Rousseau had some ideas about that too, of course, which I have discussed at length in my essay on civil religion.[33]

Wrestling with Freedom

The rapid rise and equally rapid fall of civil marriage, as something both distinct and separate from religious marriage, is a symptom of our politically cultivated alienation from religion and theology. In the recent controversy I have been hesitant to say much about religion, for the simple reason that the debate about same-sex marriage has featured so many non sequiturs and so many specious arguments – every one of them a danger to our children – that it was necessary first of all to rush to the defence of reason rather than of religion. But the two are related, and their well-being mutually dependent, as John Paul II rightly reminded us in *Fides et Ratio*. Moreover, as Witte has so convincingly shown, we cannot discuss marriage intelligently, from a legal standpoint or any other, without reference to religion.[34] That is the view of DeCoste as well, who highlights one vital reason: "The project of modest governance is impossible to conceive without the sorts of persons marked by the self-conception that religion makes possible ... [M]odest governance, limited government, requires subjects who conceive of themselves as independent from the state and who seek their spiritual and material ends, not through and in the state, but by means of the institutions, the patrimony of private life, which exist beyond the state."

"Faith and family," says DeCoste, "are central to the project of liberal governance. They are the sites most subversive of the tendency of states to imperial expansion and despotic consolidation. And they are this both because they are, by nature and stature, the practices most removed from the spirit of politics and because each is, for that very reason, a foundry in which persons of the sort required for limited government are alone to be formed."[35] What the Supreme Court's *distinctio et separatio* between civil and religious marriage demonstrates is that the Canadian state is no longer interested in these foundries. How far it is the state's task to stoke the fires even of the family foundry may be argued. But a state that is busy quenching those fires is a state that no longer knows the meaning of the word "liberal," a state that aspires to tyranny. The task of illuminating marriage in the present context must therefore be a task of demonstrating its link to freedom, and of reversing first the Rousseauvian assumptions and then some of the Rawlsian assumptions as well. Toward that end I want to offer a few further thoughts, unabashedly theological.[36]

In *The City of God*, book 22, chapter 17, Augustine is considering whether in the resurrection women will rise from the dead with their own gendered body. He insists that the female gender is not a defect but that human sexual complementarity belongs to God's good creation, and concludes that gender will not be eradicated, even though sexual relations as such will be transcended in that final blessedness. This leads him to reflect for a moment both on Genesis 2 and on Ephesians 5; that is, on the biblical paradigm of Adam and Eve and on Saint Paul's doctrine of Christian marriage as a mystery that witnesses to the loving and fecund union between Christ and the church. He points out that the Latin text of Genesis uses a very Pauline term to refer to the construction of Eve from the rib of Adam: God "built up" (*aedificavit*) Eve out of Adam, distinct yet united, subsequent but not inferior, just as God builds up or edifies the church out of Christ and for Christ: a new Eve for the new Adam, from whose side, pierced by a spear, there pours forth water and blood, signifying the grace of baptism and of the Eucharist. In other words, marriage is grounded protologically in the created order, and eschatologically in the *ordo salutis*. It serves creation and it may serve redemption. It is caught up, with the church, in the covenantal character of the relation between God and Israel, which is for the salvation of the nations.[37]

On this perspective, marriage is greatly dignified, as Leo XIII observes at the outset of *Arcanum Divinum* (1880). Yet it is not idolized. Men and women may become immortal, but marriages may not. Only the marriage of Christ and the church is eternal. Human marriage (though a higher good than the state) is a relative good, not an absolute good; virginity for the sake of the gospel is also a good.[38] As for bastards, no one is a bastard who has God as Father and the church as mother.[39]

Michelangelo's rendition of the Holy Family, the *Doni tondo*, which hangs in the Uffizi and is reproduced on the cover of this book, affords a glimpse of the dignity that Christianity has lent to marriage. It is worth pausing over for a moment, for it deliberately projects the newly elevated institution against the backdrop of pagan society[40] and the imperfections of the family – imperfections so poignantly portrayed by Augustine, with Tully's help, in *City of God* book 19, chapter 5. Marriage itself has been baptized, so that through it the society of the family may now hint at something like an *imago Trinitatis*, a union in communion. Which is to say, it is opened up to the new ecclesial reality that is destined for eternal peace; by grace it is permitted to partake, in its way, of the nature of the church.

Pre-Christian depictions of the family never attain anything quite like this. The three goods of marriage in the Augustinian tradition stand forth powerfully: *proles*, or procreation, in the young child held aloft; *fides*, or faithfulness, not least in the concentrated look on Joseph's face; *sacramentum*, or the mystery of union, in the harmony of Mary and Joseph that is mediated by Jesus. Yet each of these goods is in turn subverted by the gospel story: the child is not the child of their union; the father is no patriarch; the sacrament of this marriage does not exist for its own sake but altogether for the sake of Christ, on whom the eyes of John, Joseph, and Mary all converge. Moreover, the trinitarian harmony, Rublev-like, serves a cruciform architecture, in which the right side of the child is exposed, as if to the thrust of the spear. The Holy Family embodies freedom from human strife, but freedom comes at a cost. And the family itself – particularly the families of the faithful – will share in that cost, as the adult Christ, himself celibate, more than once reminded his disciples.[41]

With the advent of the Holy Family, new depths of meaning

and new possibilities have been disclosed for marriage and the family. At the same time marriage and the family have been transcended. Something similar might be said (were we to speak also about the resurrection) with respect to civil society and the state. They have been given a new lease on life but have also been confronted with quite definite limits. The institution of marriage has had a hand in this. Christianly conceived, marriage is both prior to the state in the natural order and *above* the state by virtue of its sacramental potential. It is a reminder to the state of its secularity, and hence of its relativity. Marriage checks the tendency of the state to overreach itself. That is one of its civil purposes.

Here is a lesson we thought we had learned. The preamble to our 1960 *Bill of Rights* (as I never tire of pointing out to my fellow citizens) affirms that "the Canadian Nation is founded upon principles that acknowledge the supremacy of God, the dignity and worth of the human person and the protection of the family in a society of free men and free institutions." Paul Martin Sr, its chief drafter, spoke at the time very much as Leo XIII might have spoken,[42] that is, of "the sanctity and inviolability of the family as the fundamental unit of society."[43] The preamble assumes that the marital or family unit is by no means a creation of the state. Marriage does not exist for the state but the state for marriage. Marriage precedes and exceeds the state, just as Christianity insists. At least on this point, then, between civil and religious marriage there may be a *distinctio* but no *separatio*. Marriage, if not a creature of the state, is not at the state's disposal; neither is the family.

The Supreme Court of Canada appears to reject all of this, however, in spite of the fact that the preamble to the 1982 *Charter* still alludes to it by linking the rule of law to belief in the supremacy of God. Not only does the court invent a separation that never before existed, it invites the government to redefine marriage along lines that include what the *Doni tondo* sets marriage over against. (Note the pointed contrast between the Holy Family and the three figures behind Joseph's back.) The court offers in explanation of its *separatio* only that Canada has become a "pluralistic" society that lacks the shared social values that attended and supported the unity between civil and religious marriage. In defence of the novelty called "same-sex marriage," it offers the *Charter* principle of equality, as if that were the product of some new consensus not indebted to Christian insight. The court's ignorance of history is lamentable, indeed inexcusable. So are the gaps and inconsistencies in its reasoning, and in its reading of contemporary Canada, but we need not revisit all of that. We may well remain puzzled as to how the meaning of marriage has been stood on its ear, but the vital question is not *how* this has happened but *where* it has happened. And the court has inadvertently supplied the answer. It has happened in what was once called Christendom.

Why has the reversal of the meaning of marriage taken place in post-Christian[44] countries and not elsewhere? Many explanations can be given, all of which are more or less cogent and none of which are unconnected to our Christian past. But I will give you what I believe to be the deepest and most important explanation.[45] Liberty and freedom have been revealed and rendered concrete in the person of Jesus Christ. Liberty and freedom have been brought into the world and placed within reach of the citizens of the nations. This has had an impact on marriage and the family, as on everything else. Though the changes have been realized only slowly and imperfectly, marriage and the family have been forever altered by the fact of the Holy Family. They have been affirmed, but they have also been transformed and transcended. Thus we who so pride ourselves on our power to choose have been given a choice that we did not have before: We can learn to understand the family in terms of the threefold marital cord (the *proles, fides, et sacramentum*) that binds it together as a communion of life, as a covenantal community and not merely a contractual one, and we can learn to penetrate the deeper ecclesial mystery that undergirds marriage and also qualifies it. Conversely, we can ignore or even resent that mystery and begin to sever the cord, strand by strand, according to the dictates of some other notion of freedom – a competing notion such as autonomy – that we have devised for ourselves by a complicated process of borrowing and perverting the true freedom that is found in Christ. It seems that we have been choosing the latter course.[46]

We are already paying dearly for this choice in a variety of ways, as some of our sociologists, economists, psychologists, and other experts acknowledge. But too seldom acknowledged is the political price we are paying. By calling on the state to reinforce our autonomy we are instead badly compromising it. In becoming a nation of bastards we are reviving the *ancien régime* from which we once were delivered, and resurrecting its oppressive Caesar-principle: *Kaisar Kyrios!* Wittingly or unwittingly, we are building up the man of lawlessness (to use Saint Paul's expression)[47] in the name of law. We are indeed "courting" Leviathan.

We cannot say that we have not been warned. Behind Ted DeCoste's warning lie many others. Pope Leo admonished us long ago that "the alteration by the state of the fundamental laws that govern marriage and family life will ultimately lead to the ruin of society itself."[48] Early in the last century men of prophetic insight, such as G. K. Chesterton and Christopher Dawson, looked ahead and foresaw our situation with remarkable clarity. Listen to Dawson, who rightly makes society share the blame: "No doubt the state will gain in power and prestige as the family declines, but state and society are not identical. In fact, the state is often most omnipotent and universal in its claims at the moment when society is dying, as we see in the last age of the Roman Empire. As the vital energy of society declined, the machinery of bureaucratic administration grew more vast and more complicated, until the wretched provincial was often glad to abandon his household and take refuge in the desert or among the barbarians in order to escape from the intolerable pressure exercised by the ubiquitous agents of the bureaucracy."[49]

Of course, the technological triumphs of the twentieth century have blinded many to the decay of our society's vital energy, the energy produced by the foundries of faith and family. That is one reason why we have been slow to see that the battle over marriage is precisely a battle over freedom, a freedom that is gradually slipping away from us. These same technological triumphs make it imperative that those who wish to preserve the foundry of the family recognize that appeals to biology and to culture, however necessary and right-minded, are inadequate.[50] The defence of marriage and the family must also be a theological defence, forged in the foundry of faith. For the institution of marriage has been placed by God (as Augustine and Michelangelo imply) on the very threshold of freedom, and freedom is ultimately a theological concern. ▩

Notes

1   Nor does the French state, apparently. The Associated Press reported
    on 4 July 2005 that the Cabinet had removed the legal distinction
    in the 1804 Napoleonic code "between a 'legitimate' child and a
    'natural' child born to unmarried parents." According to the same
    report nearly half of French babies are now born out of wedlock.
    On the other hand, the *Report on the Family and the Rights of
    Children* (French National Assembly, 25 January 2006) represents a
    serious effort to recover some of the traditional concerns of marriage.

2   I use the term "covenant" not to refer specifically to the Calvinist
    model, but to refer more generally to that which distinguishes what
    Witte identifies as the Catholic, Lutheran, Calvinist, and Anglican
    models from the contractarian model. The main distinguishing
    feature appears in his concluding reflections in the form of a
    recognition that "both Catholic and Protestant traditions have seen
    that marriage is at once a natural, religious, social, and contractual
    unit; that in order to survive and flourish, this institution must be
    governed both externally by legal authorities and internally by moral
    authorities" (John Witte Jr, *From Sacrament to Contract: Marriage,
    Religion, and Law in the Western Tradition*, Louisville, Westminster
    John Knox Press, 1997, 217).

3   F. C. DeCoste, "Courting Leviathan: Limited Government and Social
    Freedom in Reference Re Same-Sex Marriage" (2005) 42 *Alberta Law
    Review* 1099-1122.

4   Cf. Farrow, ed., *Recognizing Religion in a Secular Society* (Montreal,
    McGill-Queen's University Press, 2004), xvi.

5   1866. L.R. 1 P. & D. 130, at p. 133; quoted at para. 21.

6   *Reference re Same-Sex Marriage*, 2004 SCC 79, para. 22.

7   Ibid., para. 24. The court might have troubled itself to consider pre-
    Christian precedent. As the third-century Roman jurist Modestinus
    famously put it: "Marriage is the union of a man and a woman, a
    consortium for the whole of life involving the communication of
    divine and human rights" (*Dig.* 23.2.1). In a lecture at Calvin College,
    Russell Hittinger comments ("What Nature Hath Taught All Animals:
    Considerations on the Nature of Marriage," 15 May 2004): "This is
    the teaching common to jurists, philosophers, and theologians: a
    sexually differentiated pair, who consent to an exclusive one-flesh
    union for the whole of life. The common tradition typically spoke

of an *interior conformatio* (a mutual moulding), and *totius vitae communio* (a blending of life as a whole), of *traditio personae* (a handing over of one person to another), and of *ius in corpus* (a right to the body, not as property but as usufruct, the fruits of a thing which can be enjoyed without destroying or impairing the thing itself). This is the natural juristic language for matrimonial union."

8   They have also misread *Hyde*'s reference to Christendom, as DeCoste points out.

9   "Lord Sankey acknowledged, at p. 134, that 'several centuries ago' it would have been understood that 'persons' [i.e., senators] should refer only to men. Several centuries ago it would have been understood that marriage should be available only to opposite-sex couples" (para. 25). The analogy is false because the change envisioned is of a different order. That the framers of the Constitution assumed that senators would be male has something to do with their understanding of gender roles, and nothing to do with their understanding of the senate qua senate. That they also assumed that marriage was between a man and a woman has to do with their understanding of marriage qua marriage, and nothing to do with their understanding of sex or gender.

10 At para. 27 the court writes: "The natural limits argument can succeed only if its proponents can identify an objective core of meaning which defines what is 'natural' in relation to marriage. Absent this, the argument is merely tautological. The only objective core which the interveners before us agree is 'natural' to marriage is that it is the voluntary union of two people to the exclusion of all others. Beyond this, views diverge. We are faced with competing opinions on what the natural limits of marriage may be." But in fact it is the *court* that is arguing tautologically. It takes the abstraction ("two persons") as a starting point, which is precisely what those who object to same-sex marriage refuse to do. Cf. Daniel Cere and Douglas Farrow, eds., *Divorcing Marriage* (Montreal, McGill-Queen's University Press, 2004), 98f.

11 For that matter, Chesterton was not wrong when he prophesied (*G.K.'s Weekly*, 19 June 1926) that "the next great heresy is going to be simply an attack on morality; and especially on sexual morality." Cf. in the same vein Christopher Dawson, "Christianity and Sex," *Enquiries into Religion and Culture* (New York, Sheed & Ward, 1936), 263ff.

12 The quotations are all from Coontz's *Newsday* article, "Pivotal Role
    of Marriage Is an Illusion" (3 May 2005), which provides the gist of
    her book, *Marriage, A History: From Obedience to Intimacy, or How
    Love Conquered Marriage* (New York, Viking Adult, 2005).

13 This is not the place to engage the sociological data. But we do know
    that, by several important standards of measurement, recordable
    outcomes for children born out of wedlock do not compare
    favourably with those of children of married couples, particularly
    with those of married couples who do not separate or divorce.
    As an article on the StatsCan Web site puts it: "The increasing
    number of common-law unions, lone-parent families and blended
    families profoundly affects the everyday life of Canada's children"
    (http://142.206.72.67/02/02d/02d_002a_e.htm).

14 The preamble to C-38, which has no binding legal force, continues
    to pretend otherwise, while holding to the same general conception
    of the nature of marriage and of the flexibility of "family" life:
    "WHEREAS marriage is a fundamental institution in Canadian
    society and the Parliament of Canada has a responsibility to support
    that institution because it strengthens commitment in relationships
    and represents the foundation of family life for many Canadians ..."

15 p. 215 (source: Friederich Merzbacher, *Liebe, Ehe, und Familie*, 1958;
    quoting a letter of 1886).

16 "There *is* a distinction that is properly at play here, but that
    distinction does not reside in the *faux* distinction, concocted by the
    judicial branch, between civil and religious marriage. The distinction
    that counts is, rather, the distinction between state and society. The
    Supreme Court, of course, hides behind its investment in the civil-
    religious distinction, in order not once to acknowledge that this is
    so. Yet, by the same means, it *does* nonetheless provide an answer to
    the law and society question, at least so far as marriage is concerned.
    That answer is this: that, as regards this form of life, the political
    has primacy over the social. Nor is this answer modestly delivered:
    because marriage has no fixed political or legal meaning, it stands
    now entirely as the handmaiden of the state, at beck and call to
    the state's always revisable interests and values." DeCoste goes on
    to indicate that "this commitment to the primordiality of political
    causation" cannot be made, "as the Court appears to think, without
    cost to the remainder of social life – and to family and religious life
    particularly" (1114f.).

17 p. 1109.
18 p. 1118.
19 Politically speaking, the controversy over marriage may be seen as a continuation of the ancient controversy over lay investiture. The church may have won that round, preserving the integrity of its clerical orders, but the state is busy exacting its revenge among the laity, as the latter follow Rousseau's advice, becoming "perfectly independent" of their fellow citizens but "excessively dependent on the republic."
20 Cf. my remarks to the Legislative Committee on Bill C-38, 38th Parliament, 1st Session, June 7, 2005.
21 *On Higher Ground* (Toronto, Stoddart, 1996), 155, quoting Alex Proudfoot; see also *The War Against the Family* (Toronto, Stoddart, 1993).
22 Cf. www.brusselsjournal.com/node/1330 and www.lifesite.net/ldn/2006/sep/060927.html.
23 European Court of Human Rights, Fifth Section, Decision as to the admissibility of application no. 35504/03 by Fritz Konrad and others against Germany, 11 September 2006 (http://www.uni-trier.de/~ievr/eng/emrk.htm: "The Law," para. 1).
24 The Germans, one notes, have an interesting approach to "integration." This very passage, which derives from the ruling of the Federal Constitutional Court, was used to justify the state kidnapping of Melissa Busekros from her family home on 1 February 2007, by some fifteen police officers and other state officials. She was detained for weeks on the trumped-up charge of "school phobia," until on her sixteenth birthday she escaped custody.
25 Lenira Haddad, "An Integrated Approach to Early Childhood Education and Care: A Preliminary Study," Childcare Resource and Research Unit, Centre for Urban and Community Studies, Occasional Paper 16, 2002, 3ff.
26 *The Cambridge Lectures 1991*, ed. Frank E. McArdle (Cowansville, Les éditions Yvon Blais), 147ff.
27 "Remarks of the Right Honourable Beverley McLachlin, Chief Justice of Canada, on the Occasion of the World Conference on Religion and Education," 29 November 2004, 17f.
28 Cf. 3, 18. Tolerance is here put where the Greeks put justice and Christians put charity, and a sorry synthesis it makes.
29 p. 18f.

30 One may also wonder whether the law can do its work of preserving religious freedom "whatever the particular legal model we inherit or choose." But is McLachlin feeling her way toward a deeper understanding of the relation between law and religion? "It may be, indeed, that the state is no more able to rid itself of the demands of faith than individuals are. More profoundly, it may be that a free and liberal state cannot be sustained by simply avoiding governmental interference with religious beliefs. In the eyes of many, some form of positive validation of the faith of citizens is necessary to make effective the constitutional promise of religious freedom" (14f.).

31 With its imaginary Central London Hatchery and Conditioning Centre.

32 One may doubt that such things follow from same-sex marriage or from the definition "a union of two persons." But few commentators – Gairdner is an exception – foresaw same-sex marriage even a decade ago. In 1930 Christopher Dawson saw this much: "[If] the primary social unit is a natural biological group which is defended by the strongest moral and religious sanctions, society can never become sheer mechanism, nor can the economic organisation of the state absorb the whole life of the citizen. If, on the other hand, marriage is transformed into a temporary arrangement for the satisfaction of the sexual impulse and for mutual companionship, which is not intended to create a permanent social unit, it is clear that the family loses its social and economic importance and that the state will take its place as the guardian and educator of the children. Society will no longer consist of a number of organisms, each of which possesses a limited autonomy, but will be one vast unity which controls the whole life of the individual citizen from the cradle to the grave" (*Enquiries* 262f.).

33 Chap. 9 in *Recognizing Religion in a Secular Society*.

34 See also e.g. Charles J. Reid Jr, "The Unavoidable Influence of Religion upon the Law of Marriage," *Quinnipiac Law Review* 23.2 (2004), 493-5-28, and *Power over the Body: Equality in the Family* (Grand Rapids, Eerdmans, 2004).

35 p. 1116.

36 I hasten to add that neither the destructive nor the constructive task can be fulfilled here, nor is that my intention. I can only point to a few of the sources and ideas to which one might appeal.

37 Marc Chagall represents this in an interesting way in his series,
    La Creation de l'Homme, in Nice's Museé de Biblique.

38 Leo XIII thus asserts in §12 of *Rerum Novarum* (1891): "In choosing
    a state of life, it is indisputable that all are at full liberty to follow
    the counsel of Jesus Christ as to observing virginity, or to bind
    themselves by the marriage tie."

39 Cf. Michael Banner, "'Who Are My Mother and My Brothers?' Marx,
    Bonhoeffer and Benedict and the Redemption of the Family," chap. 7
    in *Christian Ethics and Contemporary Moral Problems* (Cambridge
    University Press, 1999).

40 *The Holy Family with the Infant St. John the Baptist*, also known as
    the *Doni tondo*, is thought to have been painted "about 1506, on the
    occasion of the birth of Agnolo Doni and Maddalena Strozzi's first
    daughter ... The nudes on the background, whose poses and gestures
    are all connected to classical sculptures, symbolize pagan mankind,
    the world before [the] coming of Christ; on the right the little saint
    John indicates the passage, through the baptism, from the pagan age
    to the christian age" (http://gallery.euroweb.hu/html/m/michelan/
    2paintin/1doniton.html).

41 See e.g. Luke 14:26f.

42 §12 of *Rerum Novarum* continues: "No human law can abolish
    the natural and original right of marriage, nor in any way limit the
    chief and principal purpose of marriage ordained by God's authority
    from the beginning: 'Increase and multiply.' Hence we have the
    family, the 'society' of a man's house – a society very small, one must
    admit, but none the less a true society, and one older than any State.
    Consequently, it has rights and duties peculiar to itself which are
    quite independent of the State."

43 See further *Divorcing Marriage* 168f.

44 "Post-Christian" is what the court really means when it says
    "pluralistic," though in fact pluralistic need not imply post-Christian.

45 For the principle at work here, cf. chap. 7 of Oliver O'Donovan, *The
    Desire of the Nations: Rediscovering the Roots of Political Theology*
    (Cambridge University Press, 1996), though O'Donovan is not
    treating the marriage issue itself.

46 Some of course have tried to reconcile the two, but it cannot be done;
    cf. Farrow, "Beyond Nature, Shy of Grace," *International Journal of
    Systematic Theology*, 5.3 (2003), 261-286.

47 Cf. 2 Thessalonians 2:3f.

48 This summary is Dawson's (*Enquiries* 267). Cf. *Arcanum* §§16-19,
which deserve to be quoted at length in the hearing of our high-court
justices and parliamentarians, especially those who demand the strict
separation of civil from religious marriage. "It is a reproach," says
Leo (§16), "to some of the ancients that they showed themselves the
enemies of marriage in many ways; but in our own age, much more
pernicious is the sin of those who would fain pervert utterly the
nature of marriage, perfect though it is, and complete in all its details
and parts. The chief reason why they act in this way is because very
many, imbued with the maxims of a false philosophy and corrupted
in morals, judge nothing so unbearable as submission and obedience;
and strive with all their might to bring about that not only individual
men, but families, also – indeed, human society itself – may in
haughty pride despise the sovereignty of God."

49 *Enquiries* 267.

50 Biological and cultural arguments about marriage can never be
fully conclusive, taken by themselves, in part because science is
on the brink of seizing control (or so it imagines) of biology and
hence also of culture. Cf. *Halpern v. Canada* (2002), O.J. no. 2714 at
para. 89: "'Procreation' – the production of offspring naturally – is
amongst the concepts affected by the evolution wrought by these
changes. Scientific advances have made it possible for children to
be born to couples – heterosexual or homosexual – through artificial
insemination, in vitro fertilization in its various forms, surrogate
motherhood, et cetera. While it remains true – at least for now – as
Justice Gonthier observed in M. v. H., that birth in a same-sex union
by necessity must involve a third person, procreation through
heterosexual coupling, as the source of the 'reality' of children being
born into a family, and therefore as the characteristic giving marriage
its principal rationale and unique heterosexual nature, is becoming
an increasingly narrow and shaky footing for the institution of
marriage." As soon as we object to this, say, that it fails to regard
the interests of children, who appear here only as a possibility
or impossibility for couples (i.e., for adults), we must add to our
biological and cultural arguments something that approaches a
theological argument, viz., a challenge to the autonomy principle
that determines the whole train of thought.

Which Secularism?

Rethinking the Role of Religion in Public Life

That things should not drift haphazard and

at random, with whole populations tossed

like waves to and fro; this, I say,

is the achievement of God's wisdom.

SAINT JOHN CHRYSOSTOM, *TWENTY-FOURTH HOMILY ON ROMANS*

TODAY we are beginning to hear voices that speak of post-secularity. The sudden (and arguably disastrous) demise in our country of the legal tradition of marriage as a monogamous heterosexual institution, in the name of secularism, suggests that we might do well to pay attention to those voices. Certainly there is something quite misleading in the oft-repeated refrain that ours is a secular country, and something profoundly wrong with the secular principles to which we are told we must do obeisance in marriage as in almost everything else.

We may begin by listening to Jürgen Habermas, who criticizes the zero-sum game that he sees being played out between the forces of anti-religious progressivists, with their appeal to scientific authorities, and religious conservatives, whose concern is with religious authorities.[1] This contest, observes Habermas, has been decided largely in favour of the former. The liberal state has thrown its weight behind the progressivists, granting to their opponents as a consolation prize the right to freedom of religion, while confining religion as such to the private sphere as a subjective matter of no direct relevance to the *res publica*. Habermas thinks it is time to stop playing this game. Under the rubric of "enlightened common sense" he has proposed a mediation between the putative objectivity of the secularist and the supposed subjectivity of the religionist. Enlightened common sense, with its emphasis on human autonomy,[2] humbles both science and religion, inviting each to listen to the other and to seek common ground in an authentically human wisdom.

My estimable McGill colleague Margaret Somerville offers a similar analysis in *The Ethical Canary* and in her recent Massey lectures, *The Ethical Imagination*.[3] She does not speak of post-secularity, and indeed takes for granted that the triumph of secularity imposes on moral reasoning, as a public exercise, the condition that it must make no direct appeal to religion. Yet in seeking a way forward she too opposes what she calls a "pure science" model to a "pure mystery" model. Rejecting both as reductionist, she proposes instead a "science-spirit" or "secular-sacred" model to overcome this unhappy dichotomy. And her mediation appears to depend, to some extent, on the validity of core religious (especially Christian) ideas about good and evil, human dignity, and the like.

To these voices others may be added, including that of H.R.H. Charles, Prince of Wales. Fear of ridicule for even mentioning God, says the prince, "is a classic indication of the loss of meaning in so-called Western civilization." Wrestling with the same underlying dualism that disturbs Habermas, he continues: "Nearly all the great religions of the world have held an integral view of the sanctity of the world. The Christian message with, for example, its deeply mystical and symbolic doctrine of the Incarnation, has been traditionally a message of the unity of the worlds of spirit and matter, and of God's manifestation in this world and humankind. But during the last three centuries ... a dangerous division has come into being in the way we perceive the world around us. Science has tried to assume a monopoly – even a tyranny – over our understanding ... Science has attempted to take over the natural world from

God, with the result that it has fragmented the cosmos and rel-egated the sacred to a separate, and secondary, compartment of our understanding, divorced from the practical day to day existence. We are only now beginning to gauge the disastrous results of this outlook."[4]

Now all of this may seem like a sign of spring to those who regard secularism as the source of some of modern society's most lamentable features. Is it not an invitation to religion to recover its public voice? Enthusiasts may be forgiven if they fall at once to arguing the toss between "enlightened common sense" or "science-spirit" terminology, or perhaps some other conceptuality, as the best way to play this new game. But I find myself, I have to confess, somewhat skeptical.

Why? Certainly not because I am opposed to religion or reli-gious discourse in the public sphere. On the contrary, I think it necessary, and more or less inevitable. I quite agree that the human being cannot be divided neatly into visible and invis-ible parts, and that human society, insofar as it seeks to confine public deliberation or public policy to the sphere of the body rather than the soul, is enormously impoverished – humanly insolvent, we might say. The Prince of Wales again: "I believe there is a growing sense of the danger of these materialist pre-sumptions in our increasingly alienated and dissatisfied world. Some may say that the tide is ... beginning to turn, but I fear there are large herds of conventional sacred cows blocking the path. Some scientists are slowly coming to realize the awe-inspiring complexity and *mystery* of the universe. But there remains a need to rediscover the bridge between what the great faiths of the world have recognized as our inner and our outer worlds, our physical and our spiritual nature. That bridge is the expression of our humanity."

One of the mysteries of the universe few of us have witnessed is herds of cows, conventional or otherwise, holding back the tide, but we may take the point. There is a kind of secularism – what I call supersessionist secularism[5] – that has as its goal the eradication of religion and the subjugation (its proponents would say "liberation") of the human spirit, so that the latter may be harnessed to projects that are entirely determined by temporal ends.[6] This is secularism with a Big Brother attitude. It is also a secularism that fears the influence of religion and wishes to prevent its public manifestation. In America it is bent on instant repairs to any real or imagined breach in the wall of separation between church and state (the removal of Roy's Rock, for example).[7] Though Canada has no doctrine of the separation of church and state, its monarch being titular head of the Church of England, Canadian culture too has been moving in this direction.[8] Indeed, our courts have been busy creating such a doctrine with the help of the *Charter*, over the dead body of Hobbes and the "dead letter," as one court put it,[9] of the *Charter* preamble, which (as we have seen) openly links belief in the rule of law to belief in the supremacy of God.

This kind of secularism, the kind that fears religion and seeks to repress it, is a secularism some people think we are now ready to leave behind. We are, so to speak, outgrowing it. Without leaving behind the Enlightenment itself we are getting over its trauma – a trauma that in Quebec came rather late, perhaps as late as the Quiet Revolution – and passing into a new, more mature phase, where we can desire and achieve enlightened common sense, a synthesis of science and spirit, a bridge between our physical and our spiritual nature. We do not need the old secularism any longer; nor (the sociologists now tell us) can we entirely trust the old secularization thesis, which posited not merely the differentiation of religious and secular spheres, but the decline of religion.[10]

Since I have no love for the dualistic and anti-religious secularism these people are rejecting, why then am I skeptical about what they are proposing? It is not just that I see rather a lot of evidence that the old secularism is still thriving. Witness, for example, the ban on headscarves, crucifixes, and yarmulkes in France's public places, a ban promulgated in the name of secularism; or the howl of outrage here in Canada (not to mention Italy and Spain) that greeted the Vatican's attempt to intervene in the marriage debate.[11] What is being put forward in place of the old secularism, I have to say, is highly unclear to me. What exactly is "spirit"? What, for that matter, is enlightened common sense? What bridge between the material and the spiritual is in view? Will it help us with difficult issues such as the marriage issue? It should not escape our notice that this sort of talk is hardly new, or that it lacked clarity and coherence in the past[12] and lacks clarity and coherence now.

In any case, secularism is not necessarily dualistic or anti-religious. Indeed, it is often portrayed as necessary, and may in fact *be* necessary, for the defence of religion from immodest and repressive forms of government, as well as for the defence of society from immodest and ambitious forms of religion. Most will agree that we still need *some* form of secularism, but which form? Perhaps, then, the moment is right for reviewing and reassessing secularist options, not for trying to get beyond secularism. I want to look at a couple of these, and to voice my support for one of them.

Liberal Secularism

Besides the militant secularism with which many are becoming fed up, there is also a more open-minded secularism that does not intend to be religion-exclusive. Its proponents are committed to church–state separation, of course, but do not necessarily believe that religion has no place at all in the public sphere. Unlike their militant counterparts, they are not trying to build a wall of separation that is a great deal higher than the one for which Jefferson originally sought a permit.[13] We may call this liberal secularism, since it is in the Lockean tradition rather than that of the skeptical *philosophes*.

Liberal secularism seeks neutrality. Among other things, that means no endorsement of religious ideas, but does not necessarily mean the eradication of all religious influence. This, after all, is a secularism that has lately come to pride itself on its pluralist and multicultural credentials. It is the secularism, say, of Canada's current chief justice, who in the *Chamberlain* decision remarked that "insistence on strict secularism does not mean that religious concerns have no place in the deliberations and decisions" of a public body. On the contrary: "Religion is an integral aspect of people's lives, and cannot be left at the boardroom door. What secularism does rule out, however, is any attempt to use the religious views of one part of the community to exclude from consideration the values of other members of the community."[14]

Liberal secularism supports goals already spelled out in Locke's *Letter on Toleration* – goals that are more modest than those of militant secularism, since there is no need here to lay claim to the whole of reality in some reductionist fashion. Liberal secularism's concern is with things temporal, without prejudice (it is claimed) to things eternal. "The commonwealth seems to me to be a society of men constituted only for the procuring, preserving, and advancing their own civil interests," says Locke. "Civil interests I call life, liberty, health, and indolency of body; and the possession of outward things, such as money, lands, houses, furniture, and the like. It is the duty of the civil magistrate, by the impartial execution of equal laws, to secure unto all the people in general and to every one of his subjects in particular the just possession of these things belonging to this life." Even such modest goals are unattainable, however, if religious or moral busybodies are forever embroiling us in public disputes, by trying to force on everyone a certain outlook or mode of life consistent with their own concept of the eternal. Hence Locke's equally familiar words: "I esteem it above all things necessary to distinguish exactly the business of civil government from that of religion and to settle the just bounds that lie between the one and the other. If this be not done, there can be no end put to the controversies that will be always arising between those that have, or at least pretend to have, on the one side, a concernment for the interest of men's souls, and, on the other side, a care of the commonwealth."

Just there, however, is the rub. How *do* we "distinguish exactly the business of civil government from that of religion and ... settle the just bounds that lie between the one and the other"? And how do we do it in a way that does not become religion-exclusive, placing religious persons or communities at a disadvantage, so belying the claim to neutrality? How do we do it in such a way that we do not, as Habermas fears, turn our liberalism into illiberalism?

Those who say – like Mr Chamberlain or Justice Saunders, the trial judge who first decided in his favour – that civil government is secular government, and make "secular" stand for "non-religious," may call themselves liberal. But the stance they take up is pretty hard to distinguish from the old-style anti-religious secularism.[15] If liberal secularism is to be distinguishable in practice from militant secularism, it cannot number among its goals the establishment of civil government, much less civil society, as a religion-free zone. That is, it cannot attempt to relegate religion to the sphere of the purely private: something to be parked at the door of the local school board office or, for that matter, of the prime minister's office.[16] That is to misunderstand religion quite fundamentally. To define secular in that way is to redefine religion too in terms the religions themselves do not recognize. It is to be anything but neutral.

I will not belabour the point, since others have done that well enough.[17] I will insist, however, that things temporal cannot be organized politically without any reference at all to things eternal. At the very least it will have to be admitted that those who attempt this import their own view of the eternal, secretly or openly, into the process. For it requires a particular understanding of the "eternal" to say that the eternal does not implicate politics, or to say that politics can be construed and conducted without implicating the eternal. Otherwise put, only on the basis of a particular kind of worldview (a self-defeating one, I would argue) can one deny that politics are imbricated in worldviews, or means in ends. One sign of this secret determination to impose such a worldview is the fact that many would-be "liberals" become more and more illiberal with each passing day, refusing to tolerate genuine difference and dissent.[18] Some even resort to a form of civil religion, which today is typically expressed by a politician, or perhaps by one of our ermined philospher-kings, talking about "Canadian values" in tones and in terms designed to make offending religious minorities fall to their knees and confess their sins. For her part, the post-secularist may be willing to seek advice or counsel about these values from real religions. But (if she is at all like my friend Margaret Somerville) she will still be quite wary of allowing the camel to get its nose too far into the tent.[19]

Well, if secular is not going to mean "non-religious," what *is* it going to mean? And if the goal of secularism is not to create a religion-free zone, what is its goal? Here we might appeal to the heavily modified liberal secularism at which William Galston, for one, is working, or to the *modus vivendi* construct of John Gray and of certain forms of communitarianism. Such an approach recognizes that we cannot easily divide up the human being, or civil society, in such a way as to hive off means from ends, the material from the spiritual, the temporal from the eternal. It recognizes that human beings need a vision of the good, and tangible forms of the good, if they are to be free to live the good life. But it does not fudge the issue by appealing to some vague or generic or eclectic spirituality in support of this freedom.[20] It recognizes instead that only real and specific communities – which are usually religious communities – can offer coherent visions of goods and goals. These communities exist prior to and in a more fundamental way than do civil society or the state. Civil society is not the tent, the flap of which it is the responsibility of the magistrates to keep closed to religious communities. Such communities are themselves the tents; the state's task is only to provide a kind of clearing in which they may be set up in a relatively orderly fashion.[21]

Secularism has here no anti-religious bias, for secular space is created by and for the prior spaces of religious and cultural communities. As David Novak puts it: "Communities are rarely if ever politically, economically, or intellectually self-sufficient. In one way or another they need to make alliances with others outside their own cultural domain, alliances in which neither party dominates the other, or in which either or both parties are forced to become some anonymous third entity." In the secular space of such alliances one is free to speak or not to speak in the name of one's god, if indeed one has a god, and one is certainly not required to recognize anyone else's god. What is sought together in this space is simply a common understanding of what is wise for a given society insofar as it must act in common. But its common action, and the programs or structures that serve that action, are carefully limited. Nor are they ever regarded as of ultimate importance. It is the communities themselves that deal in matters of ultimate importance. Even democratically established goals, says Novak, "cease to be democratic when they are made into anything more than penultimate temporal ends."[22]

I like this. The secular overlaps with the religious without itself supplanting or sublating the religious. It is no more, or at least not much more, than a kind of "common room" in which people of different traditions can work together on matters of mutual interest and responsibility. I have a caveat, however. It is good to aim at a limited secular space and a modest servant state. But how limited must that space be, how minimalist must be the state that operates therein, if the latter is not to embrace – at least not as a matter of principle – any good except for the good of its communities of goods? And how will the state know what makes for the good of its communities of goods, unless it too knows something about the good? How will it know, for example, whether a war is just, or whether it matters whether or not it is just? How will it know whether marriage should be heterosexual or homosexual, monogamous or polygamous or polyamorous, or whether marriage matters as a public institution?

The ongoing crisis over the definition of marriage is a major symptom of our problem here. Should the state force a change, as it has in Canada, out of concern for the dignity of homosexuals, or should it hold the line, as it has thus far in France or Australia, out of concern for religious freedom and the welfare of children? (What is this if not a concern with souls?) Should it get out of marriage altogether, as if marriage had nothing to do with "life, liberty, health, and indolency of body," or even with "the possession of outward things, such as money, lands, houses, furniture, and the like"? To settle such questions must it not resort to something like Habermas's enlightened common sense after all? Surely civil society and the state need a positive foundation as well as a clear limiting criterion – something capable of supporting a political conscience. Where are these things going to come from, if not from religion? But whose religion?

Novak leaves something of a mystery here. A satisfactory understanding of social goods and political order cannot come from Aristotle and Kant alone, he indicates, nor are such classical sources lacking in religious elements; yet that understanding can somehow be separated, for public purposes, from the religious foundations on which it is built. My guess is that this mystery might, with some effort, be cleared up in a more or less satisfactory manner. Galston, however, faces us with a more difficult challenge. Is it not the case, he asks, that democratic pluralism rests on value pluralism, and that value pluralism is not entirely consistent with a "monist" worldview? Which implies a further question, albeit one that Galston leaves unasked: Can those religions that aim at conformity to universal truth really embrace political pluralism, and can political pluralism really embrace those religions?[23]

To raise such questions is something that Rawlsian liberalism prefers not to do. The main problem of much *modus vivendi* liberalism, however, may be the same as that of a more Rawlsian variety, viz., that it remains too Lockean. That is, it quietly presupposes a broadly Judeo-Christian worldview, translated into the language of human rights, as a basic foundation, thus permitting the illusion that temporal government need have no concernment for souls and need not engage itself with spiritual issues at all – that it can therefore restrict itself in the necessary way, or at least permit itself to be restricted, if not by its religious communities then by its courts. (I say "by its courts" because the latter have been busy taking over both the positive and the negative function of the religious communities ever since the aforementioned translation was begun; and because it is increasingly evident that in North America there is room for only one such public conscience, the judiciary, and in Canada only one holy writ, the *Charter of Rights and Freedoms*.[24]) The Judeo-Christian worldview cannot be taken for granted any more, however, as nearly everyone will admit. And without it the language of human rights is highly unstable, if not actually hollow. Even where it is insisted upon, it is less than obvious what it means or to whom it applies. Increasingly its application is being settled by power games, conducted in the academy and the media and the courts and the United Nations, on behalf of the clients of worldviews more or less antithetical to those of the founding traditions, and indeed to each other. This makes our secular space much more problematic.

Once again, these difficulties will hardly be solved by post-secularity, which still presupposes some master worldview, supra- or quasi-religious, that can inform public as well as private decisions with its eclectic spiritual wisdom. This too is an illusion; no such thing exists. Have we exhausted the possibilities, then? Actually there is another possibility that has not yet been considered. It also derives from Christianity, but from a more robust Christianity than that of Locke. To suggest that we consider it is a bit risky, for it sometimes seems that the framers of modern Quebec, of modern Canada, of the European Union – and perhaps the recently converted Habermasians too – still have not grown up enough to get over the trauma of the West's coming of age, and so don't like to hear too much from a community they insist on treating as a resented ex-guardian. Be that as it may, Christianity may know a thing or two about the secular, since it was Christianity that invented the concept.

Christian Secularism

In order to get at this Christian concept of the secular we have to go beyond the sophisticated, but still inadequate, analysis of José Casanova. Seven years prior to Habermas's 2001 lecture, Casanova invited Habermas and his followers to reconsider the role religion might play "in the reconstitution of the public sphere." In *Public Religions in the Modern World* he spoke of the privatization of religion as a passing phase, and argued "that the age of secular-religious cleavages, of struggles over the historical process of modern secularization, has basically come to an end in the historical area of Western Christendom."[25] Casanova was not positing the so-called return of the sacred; that is, anticipating a search for deeper meaning after a period of demystification. He was analyzing actual developments in societies affected by Christianity. But the de-privatization he documented, which contradicted the secularist assumption that religious belief and influence must continue to wane, did not contradict belief in secularization as a process of differentiation into autonomous spheres – meaning the emancipation of the state and the economy, together with science, law, education, art, etc., from religion. A proper understanding of the secular, he claimed, even from a (contemporary) Christian point of view, is one that embraces this differentiation and respects this autonomy.

This may be a mistake, however, depending on what is meant by autonomy. Differentiation is a process of which Christianity approves in principle, and for which its own ancient "doctrine of the two" and, later, its scholastic movements were largely responsible. Moreover, the kind of differentiation to which Christianity is committed affords the highest possible respect for autonomy, since one of the pillars on which it rests is the notion of *creatio ex nihilo*.[26] But differentiation presupposes integration, and autonomy heteronomy. The concept of the secular proper to Christianity does not fail to respect the autonomy of the various spheres, then, but neither does it fail to relativize them to its primitive confession and organizing principle, "Jesus is Lord."[27] This principle embraces all of the spheres without exception. It is therefore a misunderstanding of Christian secularity to think that autonomy can serve as its main principle, or that autonomy can mean "emancipation from religion" in the sense commonly intended today, which implies that activities in these spheres should be conducted as if there were no higher truth than their own truth, or than such "truth" as we choose to invest in them.

What is the main principle of Christian secularism? Casanova himself began by recognizing that principle for what it is;

namely, an eschatological one.[28] In its original Christian sense, secular means "pertaining to the present age" – to the *saeculum* – rather than to the age to come. If that in turn demands a distinction between the secular and the religious, it certainly does not imply any cleavage or opposition, for the religious is that which mediates between the present age and the age to come. The religious permits the secular, which is already ordered indirectly to the kingdom of God – the good conduct of life here and now being a condition and a form of preparation for that kingdom – to become more directly ordered by sacramental or supernatural means. Thus the fundamental contrast is not between the religious and the secular at all, but between a passing or provisional era and the kingdom that "shall have no end."[29] On this scheme, it is only within the provisional era as such that the distinction between the religious and the secular can even arise, and (as Casanova notes) that distinction is itself mediated by the church.[30]

Through the Protestant theology that began to question the means and manner of the church's mediation, however, and through the Enlightenment philosophy that began to question, if not the promise of the kingdom itself, then the means and manner of its advent, this Christian understanding of the secular eventually gave way to a post-Christian understanding. In the latter, only the distinction between the religious and the secular remained, and that distinction – no longer mediated by the church, which was now confined to a separate sphere – began to take on the nature of an opposition. Casanova's own point is that the opposition is not strictly necessary. So long as the church is prepared to recognize the principle of autonomy, and so long as it is prepared to incorporate "as its own" the main aspects (cosmological, epistemological, and aesthetic) of the Enlightenment's critique of religion, it may join in the modern project of the practical rationalization of human life. Together with other religious partners it may even help to disclose the shortcomings in that process and "the failure of the Enlightenment to redeem its own promises," thus resisting the dangerous march of "the capitalist market and the administrative state" toward a dehumanizing world system.[31] Subject to the principle of differentiation and autonomy, it may take up once again something of a mediatorial role, then; only what it mediates to secular society will be the latter's own highest and best self-understanding.

Now what Casanova is trying to reckon with here is an inalienable feature of Christianity's eschatological approach to secularity. Christianity understands the concept of secularity precisely as a principle of modesty, even if it hasn't always lived by that modesty itself. The present age, it insists, contains nothing final or ultimate except the promise of the gospel itself. Politicians and judges, and clerics too, must not imagine that they are competent to introduce true freedom and peace on earth. That is sheer hubris and self-deception. Lacking the competence for that, they also lack the authority to attempt it.[32] This side of the second coming, their vocation is a simpler one: to uphold as far as possible, in view of the freedom and peace that God's Christ will someday introduce, a public order that discourages no one from pursuing a life of preparation for that ultimate good.

Casanova, however, appears content to ignore most of this, since it does not conform to Enlightenment canons. Nor, we may add, does it conform to the canons of pluralism with which the post-Enlightenment tradition increasingly works. What limits the pluralist or multicultural state is not its lack of competence fully to achieve the good, or the fact that it is awaiting divine judgment, but rather the fact that the society of which it is an expression is unable to agree on a common vision of the good. Indeed, it is not only unable to agree but has determined not to attempt agreement, since agreement (it supposes) can only mean repression of difference and of dissent.[33] And this necessarily limits its constituent communities too. The church must not speak to society or to the state as if they might possibly choose to conform to the Christian vision of the good or pay any heed to its eschatology. The church (like the synagogue or the mosque) must play by the rules. Any modesty it enjoins must be the modesty that civil society and the state already understand. It dare not tell them, for example, that they lack authority to declare marriage to be whatever they want it to be, or to deny personhood to fetuses, or to experiment on embryos. On the prevailing liberal view, that is what "secularity" implies.

The more robust Christianity of which I spoke does not accept these rules. It reserves its right to speak directly to individuals, to other communities, to society at large, and to the state too, in contradiction (if need be) of their own self-understandings. In other words, it does not accept the terms of Casanova's solution to the secularization debate, a solution it can only see as an endorsement of Enlightenment eschatology over against Christian eschatology, or else as a refusal of all public eschatology. It recommends a different kind of secularism, one that knows something about *relating* temporal and eternal ends, as well as about distinguishing them. Its own approach to secularism – based as it is on an expectation of divine judgment and salvation – is capable of just that, for what is judged is held accountable to a standard. It is neither confused with that standard nor set free from it; hence it is held responsible. But it is held responsible in genuine hope and expectation. The same cannot be said of the Enlightenment approach, which reduces (as Kant knew) to a principle of perpetual critique, such that the never-ending postponement of the good must sooner or later begin to call the good into question.[34] Nor can it be said of the pluralist approach, which cannot even begin to tell us how to govern, because knowledge of how to govern is dependent on knowledge of the good, and shared knowledge of the good is (on that view) just what is lacking.

Looked at another way, of course, this is just what is objectionable about Christian secularism. Christian secularism points out, not only that the Enlightenment *sometimes* fails to deliver on its promise, but that it cannot deliver. The principle of perpetual critique, it reminds us, can never lead to the situation of perpetual peace; nor can the pluralist principle. Either, if pressed, leads only to the "procedural republic" that is all regulation and no righteousness – all law, if you please, and no Torah. Progress toward the procedural republic is not progress in human freedom or in human happiness, any more than the end of monogamous heterosexual marriage as a privileged institution (which is one of its present demands) is the end of the war against the family. But to those heavily invested in that direction the warning may not be a welcome one.

More positively, Christian secularism calls for a political life that is both empowered and restrained by knowledge of the good.[35] It thus positions itself beyond both Rawlsian and *modus vivendi* versions of liberal secularism. The former eschews the public political significance of comprehensive visions of the good, and demands that everyone do so: a dubious manoeuvre that relies on the borrowed capital of an "overlapping consensus" that is rapidly disappearing, while looking suspiciously like a bid for the hegemony of one particular comprehensive vision.[36] The latter, in order to make room politically for comprehensive visions, calls into question the possibility of substantial consensus between communities. Christian secularism always hopes for such a consensus, and always works toward it, but does not propose to arrive at it by avoidance of religious beliefs or of comprehensive visions of the good – much less by taking refuge in the vagaries of post-secularity. Christian secularism, just because it is eschatological before it is philosophical or political, is committed to transparency in such things. In so far as it remains true to its eschatological frame of reference, it is committed to the politics of persuasion rather than to the politics of force. It really does believe in persuasion. It is not cynical about truth, or about the priority and necessity of both truth and goodness in politics. Yet it teaches that truth and goodness, in politics as elsewhere, require the modesty and restraint of those who know themselves to be accountable both to God and to man.

These are among the reasons why it commends itself, I believe, as an answer to the question, Which secularism? That Christian secularism *is* Christian need not – indeed, ought not – be held against it. For Christian secularism is amenable and open to working on common solutions (such as that proposed by Novak, for example, whose starting point is Jewish rather than Christian). It is not a secularism that favours Christians, as if in reaction to the militant secularism that disadvantages Christians and Jews and religious people generally. It is a secularism for the whole society, a secularism that supports a modest but functional state and a body politic that takes some acount of the spiritual as well as of the material dimensions of human life. It goes without saying, however, that this secularism is not sustainable without a degree of openness to Christianity and the resources it brings to bear. Where that openness does not exist, the question "Which secularism?" will have to find a different answer. It may be doubted, however, whether it will find a better one. ▓

Notes

1   Lecture of 14 October 2001 (*Frankfurter Rundschau*, 16 October 2001, no. 240, p. 18).

2   In Kant's famous words: "Enlightenment is man's leaving his self-caused immaturity. Immaturity is the incapacity to use one's intelligence without the guidance of another."

3   Toronto, Viking, 2000.

4   "A Sense of the Sacred: Building Bridges Between Islam and the West," *The Wilton Park Seminar*, 13 December 1996.

5   See Farrow, "Three Meanings of Secular," *First Things* 133 (May 2003), 20-23, for a simple typology of secularism.

6   It is the kind of secularism represented in Britain by the National Secular Society, whose founder, George Jacob Holyoake, coined the term in the mid-1800s. The NSS asserts "that supernaturalism is based upon ignorance and is the historic enemy of progress"; it must therefore be treated as such. See Iain T. Benson, "Considering Secularism," in *Recognizing Religion in a Secular Society*, ed. D. Farrow (Montreal, McGill-Queen's University Press, 2004).

7   Such militant secularism may present itself as a defender of religious liberty, but the disguise is a thin one, and the McCarthyite approach evident enough. For an account of the history of secularism in the USA, see *The Secular Revolution*, ed. Christian Smith (Berkeley, University of California Press, 2003). On the controversy over the statue of Moses at the Alabama Supreme Court, dubbed "Roy's Rock" after ex-chief justice Roy Moore, see my "Behold the Armies of the Lord" (*Globe and Mail*, 22 August 2003).

8   Witness what took place in Ottawa after 9-11, when both the

living and the dead had to be remembered in a silence unbroken
by any appeal to the mercy of God.

9   See David Brown, "Freedom From or Freedom For? Religion as a
    Case Study in Defining the Content of *Charter* Rights," *U.B.C. Law
    Review*, vol. 33, 2000, 562, re: *R.* v. *Sharpe*, 1999, B.C.J. no. 1555, §78-80.

10 See José Casanova, *Public Religions in the Modern World*
    (University of Chicago, 1994).

11 See the CDF's "Considerations Regarding Proposals to Give Legal
    Recognition to Unions Between Homosexual Persons," 3 June 2003.

12 I am thinking of Teilhard de Chardin, for example, on whom see my
    Ascension and Ecclesia (Edinburgh, T. & T. Clark, 1999), 198ff.

13 That permit was never officially granted, but in the 1940s (esp.
    Everson v. *Board of Education, 1947*) the U.S. Supreme Court
    began to act as if it had been, and to interpret its terms in new
    and expansive ways. See John Witte Jr, *Religion and the American
    Constitutional Experiment* (Boulder, Westview, 2000), chap. 8.

14 McLachlin C.J., writing for the majority in *Chamberlain* v. *Surrey
    School District no. 36* (2002 SCC 86), at §19.

15 Cf. Gonthier J.'s dissent in the SCC's *Chamberlain* judgment (§137).
    Here it may be remarked that much of the litigation that takes place
    today in the name of liberal neutrality, *Chamberlain* itself being a
    case in point, looks rather more like the socially paralyzing action of
    Locke's moral busybodies than does anything done by most of those
    litigated against.

16 Prime Minister Martin's meeting with the Dalai Lama, we may
    assume, was held behind closed doors at Archbishop Gervais'
    residence, rather than the PM's, because of sensitivity to the Chinese,
    not to the secularists.

17 See e.g. Michael Sandel, *Liberalism and the Limits of Justice* (2nd ed.,
    Cambridge University Press, 1998).

18 Thus, for example, the recent California statute universalizing
    abortion training in obstetrics programs. What can be the effect
    of that, if not to root out of this key profession those who do not
    conform to contemporary liberal canons: those whose worldview
    compels them to recognize a higher good than "toleration," a higher
    freedom than "freedom to choose," a higher justice than "equal
    opportunity" – in short, who represent an alternative?

19 In her musings on the marriage question, Somerville likes to

draw a distinction between opposing same-sex "marriage" for secular reasons and for religious ones. As public reasons the former are fine, whereas the latter are illegitimate (see her essay in *Divorcing Marriage*, ed. D. Cere and D. Farrow, McGill-Queen's, 2004). Religious reasons may be privately held, but they may not be factored into our corporate social decisions or public policy. What may be factored in is "spirit" or "wisdom" or "values" that have in part derived from religion.

20 The kind, for instance, that reduces the doctrine of the incarnation to a symbol "of God's manifestation in this world and in humankind."

21 See further *Recognizing Religion*, chaps. 3, 4, and 8.

22 See *Recognizing Religion*, 64f., and D. Novak, "Religious Communities, Secular Society, and Sexuality: One Jewish Opinion," in *Sexual Orientation and Human Rights in American Religious Discourse*, ed. S. Olyan and M. Nussbaum (Oxford University Press, 1998), 13f.

23 Galston thinks that pluralism should make every possible allowance for such religions (granting conduct exemptions, for example, where general laws might impede religious practice), but it is not obvious that the underlying value-pluralism can have any other effect than to ghettoize their communities.

24 "If relativism is our secular religion, judges our high priests, then the Charter of Rights is our holy writ. In meaningless generalities, the Charter enunciates rights and then empowers the courts to tell us what they mean" (Ian Hunter, *National Post*, 27 November 2003).

25 p. 220; cf. 231f.

26 Scotus, and especially Ockham, made mistakes here, however, which set subsequent thinkers on the wrong track.

27 Cf. e.g. 1 Corinthians 8:6, Colossians 1:15ff.

28 See 12ff.

29 As Oliver O'Donovan remarks in *The Desire of the Nations* (Cambridge University Press, 1996), 211, "the corresponding term to 'secular' is not 'sacred', nor 'spiritual', but 'eternal'."

30 Which had (and has) secular as well as religious orders, it may be added.

31 See 229ff. In order to do this, however, the church's sphere of influence must be the sphere of civil discourse only. As a partner and friend to civil society (which is the carrier of ethical traditions)

religion maintains an important relation to politics, but its influence is indirect. It may serve to stiffen civil resistance to the state's tendency to self-aggrandizement, but it may not become directly involved with the activity of the state.

32 It is by overreaching that they turn these liberal ideals into illiberal ones; cf. O'Donovan, *Desire of the Nations*, chap. 7.

33 Pluralism itself, as an ideological tool in the hands of the state or of the media, often leads (in combination with equality-rights arguments) to repression of difference and of dissent. Witness, for example, the official demand for resignations from B.C. marriage commissioners unwilling to perform same-sex ceremonies.

34 I am, of course, reversing the charge laid against Christianity by certain of its Enlightenment critics, and by those who invented the so-called "crisis of the delay of the parousia."

35 This broad claim obviously requires more support than I can give sit here; see e.g. Augustine, *Trinity* book 13 and *City of God* book 19.

36 One that supports a political theory that sanctions state enforcement of so-called liberal neutrality, while rejecting state enforcement of any other political arrangement. Rawls's claim in *Political Liberalism* (New York, Columbia University Press, 1993) that his scheme is independent of any comprehensive view is false.

Epilogue

AS it happened, I finished my revisions to this book on la Fête de la Saint-Jean Baptiste, which for some reason the Anglicans had decided to celebrate by gathering in Winnipeg for their triennial row over same-sex unions. Switching off the radio, without even waiting for the strains of "She Flies On" to die away, I fell into a little reverie on the Doni tondo. What if it were being painted today for some wealthy Anglican patron? The preliminary sketches would surely be greeted with great puzzlement, if not undisguised dismay. For nothing could be more out of step with the spirit of our time than this bold rendition of the Holy Family.

In my reverie, changes were indeed proposed by the wealthy Anglican patron, after he had pondered the sketches awhile. Could we not have in the background, he asked, a more positive portrayal of alternative family structures? And must the Holy Family have its back to these structures? Must there be that little wall of partition, with even John on the other side? Wouldn't it be better if everyone were on equal footing, so to say?

The artist replied, as politely as possible, that to carry out such changes he would have to sacrifice his compositional analogues of core Christian doctrines – in short, abandon his trinitarian and cruciform scheme – and he didn't want to do that.

His patron, however, was unimpressed. Ours is not a theological age, he remarked, and theological insularity is particularly despised.

The artist protested that insularity was not at all what he had in mind. *Freedom* was what he had in mind. What could be freer than the freedom of the Almighty to become a babe in arms? What could be freer than the freedom of the divine Love to trace its own image in humanity? What could be less insular than the Holy Family, through which Love came to liberate humankind?

But his patron had already moved on to another problem: the Madonna. She was too prominent, and her prominence worried him. Was she really the right subject through which to reach the woman of today? It had been some time, he thought, since any popular slogan had begun with *Fiat mihi*. Today's woman, in any case, was much more interested in having sex without having a child than in having a child without having sex. Anglicans, he added proudly, had cottoned to that already in 1930. Besides, today's woman could have it either way, according to her preference. It was up to her, really, and high time too! Would the artist think him irreverent if he suggested that the painting might make a still bolder statement by recasting Joseph as B.B.?

The artist had heard of B.B., but admitted to some confusion. He observed that the patron himself was about to be married, and that to a woman. Was the commission not in honour of the occasion?

Well, yes, of course, came the slightly irritated reply. But she was a prominent banker, he the president of a burgeoning fabric company. If their lives were to be woven together, it would be around romance and finance, not the bearing and rearing of children. No children – at least not for a while. Too busy for that sort of thing.

With a wry smile, the artist pointed to his sketch and observed that the Madonna looked quite capable of handling a child on top of everything else. Glancing at his patron, who did not appear amused, the artist decided to appeal to the deeper dimensions of his art. He pulled out photos of an ancient cameo and of a round relief that had once resided in the home of Lorenzo the Magnificent. Both showed a satyr, sitting with head bowed down to his precious harvest of figs, with the infant Dionysus perched on his shoulder. The unexpected similarities to the artist's Madonna served a still more striking dissonance. The Madonna was supple and strong, like the satyr, but unlike the satyr she was not in thrall to her passions. Her head was lifted up, not bowed down. She was majestic in her serenity, and glorious in her freedom to love. The Child on her shoulder was a gift, not a burden; ever the emancipator, never the enslaver. The husband who was handing the Child to her was likewise a figure of great dignity and devotion. There was no hint of domination in either direction. For between the two there was a third – the very Source of love – and between the three there was communion.

The patron struggled to grasp what the artist was trying to show him. But the furrows in his brow only briefly mirrored the study in concentration that was Joseph. A look of resignation passed over his face. I'm an Anglican, he said at last. You can't really expect me to go back there, can you?

The artist laid down his photographs on a pile of old books with half-forgotten Latin titles. He pointed again to one of his sketches and picked out the figure of John with his forefinger. No, he said, but it seemed he was speaking more to himself than to the patron. You can't go back. You can only go forward.

When I returned from my reverie, I switched on the radio again and learned that same-sex unions were on hold for another three years. The Anglicans had decided that you can't go back and you can't go forward either. That, I concluded, is what made them Anglicans. But what could the artist have meant? Plainly not that his painting was an anachronism with nothing to say to the modern man or woman.

I stared at a reproduction of the Doni tondo and tried to recall everything I knew about John, beside the fact that he haunted the banks of the Jordan, not the Red or the Assiniboine, and wouldn't have known the words to "She Flies On." I remembered, of course, that Jesus had said of him that none greater had ever been born of woman, and yet that the least of those who entered the kingdom would be greater than he. Looking at John gazing up at Jesus from behind that little retaining wall, it occurred to me that perhaps Jesus had said this because it had been given to John to stand alone, by the river of destiny, as a signpost to us all that we have reached the point of no return. Our Liberator has come and the status quo ante is gone. The old options no longer exist.

I wondered what this might mean in the matter of marriage, an estate that neither John nor Jesus entered, though John lost his head over it. And it seemed to me that there could be no going back in the matter of marriage either, because through the Holy Family marriage itself has become what it never was before. It has become a sign of something eternally higher and better. It has become a witness to the possibility of human communion with God, the author of life; that is, to the mystery of the union of the church with Christ, the prince of life.

A book title floated into my mind, unbidden, on the flood of these reflections: *How Love Conquered Marriage*, or something to that effect. Its author seemed to think the Industrial Revolution a much more significant event than the birth of John or of Jesus. It would be hard to be much more mistaken than that. But of course Love *has* conquered marriage, hasn't it? Both for the married and the unmarried. And for that reason, there can be no going back.

The *Doni tondo* now took on fresh meaning for me, as did the essays I'd been working on. Our society is trying as hard as it can to return to what is behind the Holy Family's back, but it can't be done. It is impossible for marriage, even civil marriage, ever to be again what it was before Christianity brought it to the altar and elevated it as Holy Matrimony. We can strike the words "one man and one woman" from our definition of marriage all right, but we cannot restore even the old, pre-Christian meaning of union or *sacramentum*. We can strike the word "two," as doubtless we will, but we cannot return to the days of simple polygamy. We can bless "committed same-sex unions" in religious rites, as various sects already do, but we cannot recover even the pagan meaning of *fides*.

No, in each case we must have something else; something that in its way, openly or secretly, is a refusal of Christian liberty, an objection to Christian freedom, which the unfreedom of pre-Christians was not. We must have gay marriage, legalized polyamory, and alternative family structures so open to "alternatives" that neither "family" nor "structure" has any obvious meaning. We must have kindergartens that confuse our children about sex, and operating theatres to carry out the mutilations that those who are most confused may seek. Moreover, we must have the assurance that, whatever we do, the gods will be quite content to bless us. Oh yes, and those newly minted moral diseases, homophobia and heterosexism, to justify the shunning of those who say otherwise.

If the Anglicans ever manage to move "forward" with Canadian society, to which they fancy themselves chaplain, they will eventually discover with the rest of us just how true it is that we can't go back. We may share our figs and pomegranates, and play "She Flies On" on our panpipes, but it will only be the shade of Dionysus who appears on our shoulder. Times really have changed, whether we know it or not. ▣

Solemnity of the Birth of Saint John the Baptist, A.D. 2007

CPSIA information can be obtained at www.ICGtesting.com
Printed in the USA
LVOW07s0045021214

416502LV00002B/381/P